CAMBRIDGE ENGLISH WORLDWIDE

Student's Book One

ANDREW LITTLEJOHN & DIANA HICKS

CAMBRIDGE
UNIVERSITY PRESS

CAMBRIDGE UNIVERSITY PRESS

Cambridge, New York, Melbourne, Madrid, Cape Town, Singapore,
São Paulo, Delhi, Dubai, Tokyo, Mexico City

Cambridge University Press
The Edinburgh Building, Cambridge CB2 8RU, UK

www.cambridge.org
Information on this title: www.cambridge.org/9780521645126

First published 1998
13th printing 2010

Printed in Dubai by Oriental Press

A catalogue record for this publication is available from the British Library

ISBN 978-0-521-64512-6 Student's Book
ISBN 978-0-521-64511-9 Workbook
ISBN 978-0-521-64508-9 Listening and Speaking Pack
ISBN 978-0-521-64510-2 Teacher's Book
ISBN 978-0-521-64509-6 Class Cassette Set

Contents

Map of *Cambridge English Worldwide 1*

What's in *Cambridge English Worldwide 1?*

Cambridge English Worldwide 1 has three parts for you, the student.
There is a Student's Book, a Workbook and a Listening and Speaking Pack.

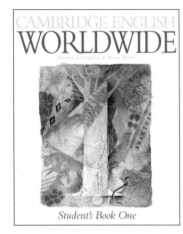

Student's Book One

Workbook One

Let's look at the Student's Book

1 Six Themes

This book has six Themes.
Match the letter to the name.
One name is not there. What is it?

Theme A	The natural world
Theme B	....
Theme C	Living history
Theme D	The way we live
Theme E	Around town
Theme F	Around the English-speaking world

2 The Themes

Look through the book.
What can you learn about in *Cambridge English Worldwide 1?*
Tell the class your ideas.

Let's look at the Workbook

3 The Workbook Units

The Workbook also has six Themes. There are two Units in each one.
What are there after Units 4, 6, 8, 10 and 12?

4 At the back

Look at the back of the Workbook. What is there?

Let's look at the Listening and Speaking Pack

The Listening and Speaking Pack has many exercises to help you.
– You can do listening exercises.
– You can talk to people on the cassette.
– You can practice your pronunciation.
– You can sing the songs!

Welcome to

CAMBRIDGE
ENGLISH
WORLDWIDE

Student's Book One

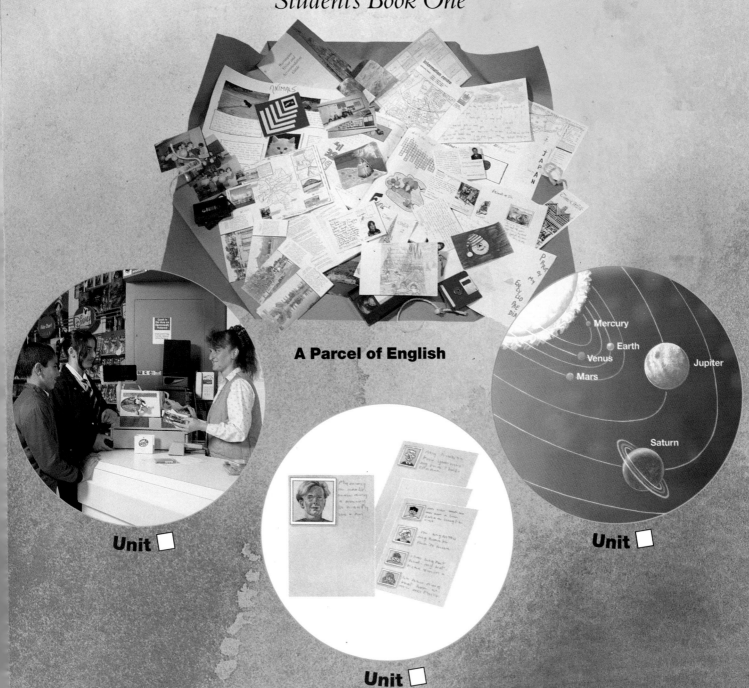

A Parcel of English

Mercury
Earth
Venus
Mars
Jupiter
Saturn

Unit ☐

Unit ☐

Unit ☐

1 Welcome to English!

1 You know a lot of English!

Look at the pictures below. Do you know the names in English?
Tell your teacher and put the words on the board.

*The English
you know*
Extra practice • WB Ex. 1

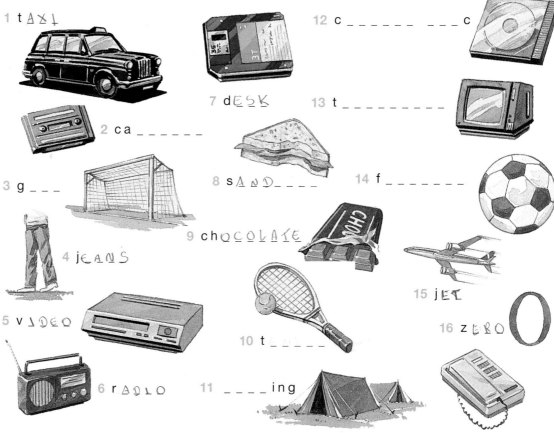

1 t A X I

2 ca _ _ _ _ _ _

3 g _ _ _

4 j E A N S

5 v I D E O

6 r A D I O

7 d E S K

8 s A N D _ _ _ _

9 ch O C O L A T E

10 t _ _ _ _ _

11 _ _ _ _ ing

12 c _ _ _ _ _ _ _ _ _ c

13 t _ _ _ _ _ _ _ _

14 f _ _ _ _ _ _ _

15 j E T

16 z E R O

17 T E L E ph O N E

What other English words and phrases do you know?

2 A puzzle

Look at the pictures again and fill in the
correct names.
What word do they make?

		2		3		6		7	8		9		10
						R							
				4		A							
1			J	5	D								
X		E		I									
A		A		O									
X		N											
I		S											

3 Hello!

 Listen to the cassette and look at the pictures.

Hello! My name is James.
I'm 12 years old.
I live in Hill Road.
I can swim very well.

Hello! My name is Martha.
I'm 13 years old.
I live in Park Road.
I can play football very well.

Who is who? Listen again.

James   Martha   Usha   Emma   Ali

I can sing very well. | I can run very well. | I can swim very well. | I can play football very well. | I can draw very well.

4 Talk about yourself

Tell the class about yourself.

 Listen to the numbers and words.

My name's Christine.
I'm 11 years old.
I live in Green Road.
I can play the trumpet very well.

10 ten	I can …	play the trumpet/piano/guitar very well.
11 eleven		draw
12 twelve		run
13 thirteen		play football
14 fourteen		swim
15 fifteen		

5 Make a poster

Draw a picture and write about yourself. Sign it with your thumbprint!

Put all your posters on your classroom wall.

The World's Greatest Football Player

Hello, my name is Sarah. I'm 14 years old.
I live in London. I can play football very well.

6 Sing a song! I'm so happy

 Listen to 'I'm so happy' and sing it with your class.
The words are on page 90.

A world trip

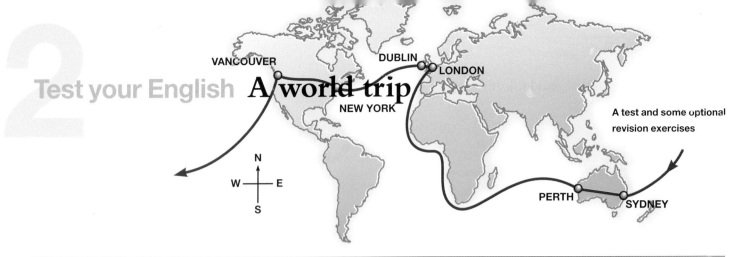

A test and some optional revision exercises

1 London to Dublin by boat

'be'

Circle the correct answer.
For example:

1. This boat ... big.
   a are b am c is

This boat ... old.
a are b am c **is**

2. I ... hot.
   a are b am c is

3. She ... hot.
   a are b am c is

4. We ... happy.
   a are b am c is

2 Dublin to New York by plane

Personal details

Complete the form about you.

JFK Airport Arrival Card

Name: .... First Language: ....

Address: .... Age: ....

.... Colour of hair: ....

Telephone number: .... Colour of eyes: ....

3 New York to Vancouver by train

Personal subject pronouns

Circle the correct answer.

1. Where are ... going?
   a you b they c it

2. ... are going to Vancouver.
   a It b He c We

3. Is that train going to Vancouver?

No, ... isn't, it's going to Toronto.
a it b he c she

4. Where are ... going?
   a he b they c it

I don't know

4 Vancouver to Sydney by land and sea

Negatives

Look at the pictures.
Circle the correct sentence.

What's the problem?

1
a I haven't got a car.
b I'm not a car.
c This isn't a car.

2
a There isn't a house.
b Here, it isn't a house.
c I haven't got a house.

3
a He isn't old.
b We don't swim.
c I'm not rich.

4
a He isn't a dog.
b I can't find my dog.
c He doesn't sleep.

5 Sydney to Perth by bus

'There is' and 'There are'

Circle the correct answer.

Let's have a quiz about Australia.

OK. Ask me some questions.

1
A: … a lot of kangaroos in Australia?
   a Are there b There are c There is
B: Yes!

2
A: … an airport in Sydney. Right or wrong?
   a Is there b There is c There are
B: Right!

3
A: … a river in Perth?
   a Is there b There are c Are there
B: Yes!

4
A: … 17 million people in Australia. Right or wrong?
   a Is there b There is c There are
B: Right!

6 Perth to London by ship

Adjectives

Circle the correct answer.

1
A: Hello Peter, how are you?
B: Fine, where are you?
A: On the ship.
B: Tell me about the ship.

A: a It's a big ship.
   b It's a small ship.
   c It's a fat ship.

2
B: I can hear music.

A: a Yes, it's modern music.
   b Yes, it's old music.
   c Yes, it's very cold music.

3
B: How is the captain?

A: a He's very green.
   b He's very long.
   c He's very fat.

4
B: Is the weather nice?

A: a Yes, it's very cold.
   b Yes, it's very hot.
   c Yes, it's very bad.

Extension **Around the world again**

Optional revision exercises

You can get more practice here on difficult things in your test.
Choose the sections you need to do.

1 You're in England. Get ready to go!

'be'

1.1 Meet Martin Wilson

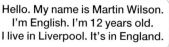

Hello. My name is Martin Wilson. I'm English. I'm 12 years old. I live in Liverpool. It's in England.

Extra practice • WB Ex. 1
Extra practice • TB Ws. 2.1

Listen to Martin.

Write sentences about yourself.

Hello.

My name …

I am …

I am …

I live …

It is …

Say your sentences to the class.

Say it clearly!

My name is …
I live …
I am …
It is …

1.2 In Liverpool

Read Martin's writing about Liverpool.

Write about your town in the same way.

Liverpool is in the north west of England. It is on the River Mersey. It is a big city. About 500,000 people live here. Liverpool has a very big port. It also has an important football team.

2 Stopover in America!

Personal details, social language

2.1 Martin Wilson arrives in New York

Extra practice • LS Ex. 1–2
Extra practice • TB Ws. 2.1

Listen. Martin is at the airport in New York. Complete the card.

JFK Airport Arrival Card

Name: Martin Wilson

Address: 25 Long Street, Liverpool

Telephone number: ....

First language: ....

Age: ....

Colour of hair: ....

Colour of eyes: ....

2.2 Your personal information

Work with a partner. Find out about your partner. Write the information on the card.

Welcome to New York.   *And your first language is …*

Can you tell me …   *What colour is …*

What's your …   *What colour are … eyes?*

How old are you?

JFK Airport Arrival Card

Name: ....

Address: ....

Telephone number: ....

First language: ....

Age: ....

Colour of hair: ....

Colour of eyes: ....

3 Stopover in Australia!

'There is / are';
adjectives

Extra practice • WB Ex. 2
Extra practice • TB Ws. 2.2

3.1 Martin sends his family a postcard

Can you label Martin's postcard?

a bridge   a port   a river
cars   trees   a park   houses
boats   tall buildings

What's in the picture? Tell the class.
You can use these words.

big old new beautiful small tall

There is a big …   There are a lot of …

There is an old …

3.2 Write part of Martin's postcard

Complete Martin's postcard.
Use the words from Exercise 3.1.

POST CARD
SYDNEY, AUSTRALIA

Dear Everyone,
I'm in Sydney. There are
a lot of people here.
Sydney has a big port.
There are ....
There is a big ....

The Wilson family,
25 Long Street,
Liverpool,
England.

3.3 A postcard of your town

Find a postcard of your town or draw a picture. Write about your town.

---

4 Stopover in India!

Negatives

Extra practice • WB Ex. 3
Extra practice • Ws. 2.2

4.1 India is very different from Australia

Read about India.   India is a very big country. There are 850 million people there. The
capital of India is New Delhi. There are 16 languages in India. There
are elephants, lions and tigers. There are also very high mountains.
India is in the Northern Hemisphere. It is near China and Pakistan.

How is it different in Australia? Write some sentences.

1. There aren't 850 million people in Australia. There are 17 million.

Useful phrases:

There isn't …   There aren't …   It isn't …

Say it clearly!

There isn't
There aren't
It isn't

4.2 Is it true?

Play a game. Work with a partner. Write down four sentences about your country,
town or school. Make some sentences true and some false.

There isn't a train station here.   There aren't many people in this city.
                It isn't very hot in our country.

Now with your class work in two teams. Say your sentences to the other team.
They say 'True' or 'False'. The first team to give 12 correct replies is the winner.

5 Welcome back to London!

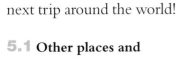

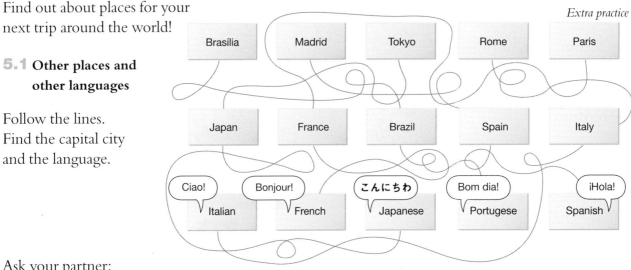

'be'; 'have'

Extra practice • WB Ex. 4

Extra practice • TB Ws. 2.3

Find out about places for your
next trip around the world!

5.1 Other places and other languages

Follow the lines.
Find the capital city
and the language.

Ask your partner:

A: *Where is Tokyo?*   B: *It's in Japan. They speak Japanese there.*

Think of some more cities and ask your partner:

A: *Where is …?*   B: *It's in … They speak … there.*

5.2 Brasília has a population of 1 million people

Listen. Choose list A or list B. Work with a partner and fill in the chart.

List A	Population
Brasília	1 million
Madrid	
Tokyo	

List B	Population
Rome	
Mexico City	
Paris	

Tell your partner your information, like this:

Brasília has a population of 1 million people.

5.3 Write part of an encyclopaedia!

Work with your partner.
Choose two cities and write
about them in the same way.

Read out your sentences to the class.
What can you say about a city in
your country?

6 Your Language Record

Now complete your *Language Record*.

AROUND THE WORLD

Brasília
Brasília is in Brazil. It has
a population of 1 million
people and they speak
Portuguese there.

Paris

Tokyo

Madrid

Mexico City

Rome

32

Language Record

Write or draw the meaning of the words. Add the missing examples.

Word	Meaning	Example
big		Liverpool is a big city.
small		
important		It has an important football team.
tall		There are many tall buildings.
beautiful		My town is very beautiful.
old		The houses are very old.
new		
long		My hair is very long.
short		

Write the meaning in your language.

Pronoun	Translation	Pronoun	Translation
I →		we →	
you →		you →	
he →		they →	
she →			
it →			

Complete the table.

I'm (I am)		We .... (...............)	
You're (you are)		You .... (...............)	very old.
He .... (...............)	English.	They .... (...............)	English.
She .... (...............)	very old.		
It .... (...............)			

Write these useful phrases in your language.

How are you? ....   Can you tell me ....

Fine, thanks. ....   How old are you? ....

Where's ....   What's your address? ....

Write some examples.

a bus station   a park   a bridge   cars   shops   restaurants

In my town, there is ....

and there are ....

Topic 3 Around our school

Town and school; curriculum links with Geography and Social Studies

1 Where is your school?

'north', 'south', 'east' and 'west'

1.1 Schools around the world

Is your school in a town or in the country?

Look at the pictures. Does your school look like one of these?
Which schools do you think are in a town?
Which schools are in the country?

1.2 Where you live

Where do you live?
In the north?
In the east?
In the south?
In the west?

David lives in the north.

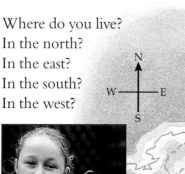

Anne and Pat live in the west.
They are friends.

LANARK

Glasgow • Edinburgh

Birmingham

NEWPORT

MILTON KEYNES

Cardiff •

London

Ali and Mona live in the south east.
They are brother and sister.

2 Near your school

Tell the class about the places near your school.

There is a park near our school.

There are some shops near our school.

There is a …

There are some …

Places near your school
Extra practice •
WB Ex. 1–2

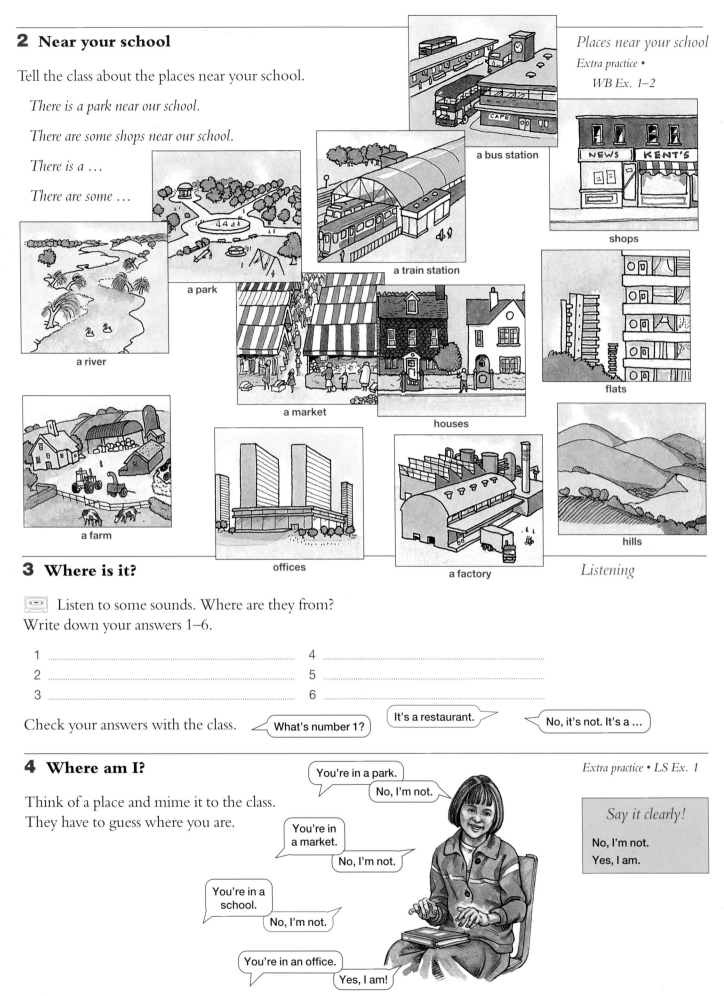

a bus station

shops

a train station

a park

flats

a river

a market

houses

a farm

offices

a factory

hills

Listening

3 Where is it?

Listen to some sounds. Where are they from?
Write down your answers 1–6.

1 ....   4 ....

2 ....   5 ....

3 ....   6 ....

Check your answers with the class.   What's number 1?   It's a restaurant.   No, it's not. It's a …

4 Where am I?

Extra practice • LS Ex. 1

Think of a place and mime it to the class.
They have to guess where you are.

You're in a park.
No, I'm not.

You're in a market.
No, I'm not.

You're in a school.
No, I'm not.

You're in an office.
Yes, I am!

Say it clearly!

No, I'm not.
Yes, I am.

5 Find the places

Reading and listening
Extra practice • WB Ex. 3
Extra practice • LS Ex. 2

Here is a letter from Anne, in Newport. Work with a neighbour.
Read the letter and look at the puzzle.
Draw lines to show where each piece goes.
Compare your answers with other students in your class.

Listen to Anne's letter.

Clifton School
Newport
Gwent
Wales

Dear Everyone,
I don't live in England, I live in Wales!
Newport is a big town in the south
of Wales. It has got a population
of 120,000 people. My school is in
the north of the town. Near the
school there are shops, offices and
cafés.
A lot of students like football. After
school they play football in the park
near the sea. I don't like football. I
go to the swimming pool near the
bus station after school. I'm in the
school swimming team.

I live about four kilometres from
school. I don't walk to school. I
go on the school bus. There
are a lot of factories near
my flat. My mother works in one
of the factories. My father
doesn't work.
On Saturday mornings I have
guitar lessons in my teacher's
house near the library and
museum.
Write and tell me about your
town and school.

Love Anne

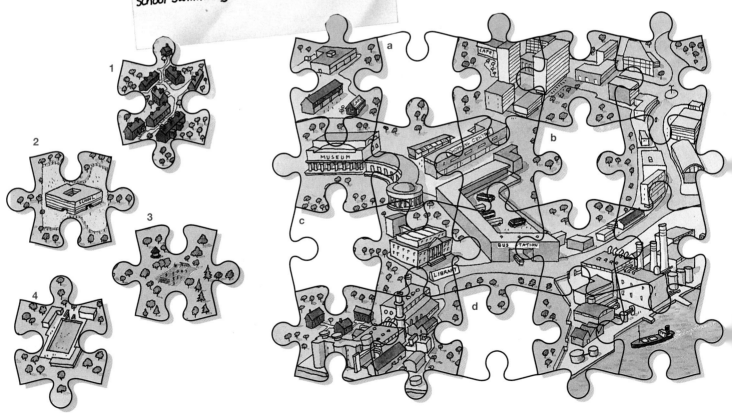

6 A favourite day

Listening and speaking

Look at Mona and Ali's new school timetable.
Do you do the same subjects at school?

🔲 Listen and find answers to these questions:

What is Mona's favourite day? What is her favourite subject?
What is Ali's favourite day? What is his favourite subject?

	Lesson	Monday	Tuesday	Wednesday	Thursday	Friday
9.00	1	English	Maths	Science	English	Art
10.00	2	Geography	Maths	Religion	English	French
11.00		Break	Break	Break	Break	Break
11.30	3	Religion	Geography	English	Geography	Sports
12.30		Lunch	Lunch	Lunch	Lunch	Lunch
13.30	4	French	Science	Maths	Sports	French
14.30	5	History	History	History	Sports	Science

Compare your answers with the rest of the class.

7 Your favourite day

*'Do you …?';
'do' and 'don't'*

Work with a partner. Look at your
own timetable. Talk about your
favourite day and favourite
subject. Say your dialogue in
front of the class.

> Hi, do you like the timetable?

> It's OK.

> What's your favourite day?

> It's …
> We have …

> What's your favourite subject?

> It's …

> Do you like …

> Yes, I do.
> No, I don't.

8 Make an exercise

Vocabulary

Can you join the parts to make seven words?
What do they mean?

stat ourite
hist table
geog raphy
time gion
reli ion
fav ject
sub ory

Find seven more words in this Unit.
Make an exercise for your neighbour.

9 Sing a song! In my town, in the countryside

🔲 Listen to 'In my town, in the countryside' and sing it with your class.
The words are on page 90.

10 Decide ...

You can work by yourself, with a partner or in a small group.
Choose an exercise.

Exercise 10.1 practises speaking and listening.
Exercise 10.2 practises writing.

Or you can do **something else**. Talk to your teacher and decide what to do.

10.1 A map game

Speaking and listening

Copy this map. Put six more things on your map.

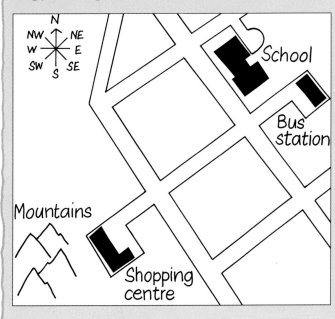

a restaurant   a factory   a river   a market   a farm
a train station   a bus station   a park   some shops
some hills   some houses   some flats   some offices

Now work with a partner.
Don't look at your partner's map.
Tell your partner where your places are.

Your partner can draw the places on his/her map.

There is a school in the north east near the bus station.

There are some shops in the south west near the mountains.

> **Say it clearly!**
>
> There's /ðeəz/
> some /sʌm/
> north /nɔːθ/
> in the south /saʊθ/

10.2 Write a letter to Anne

Writing

Read Anne's letter in Exercise 5 again.
Write to Anne and tell her where you live.

Dear Anne,
Thanks for your letter. We live in...... It is a....... It has got...... Our school is.......There are........near the school. In the street there are.......We haven't got.... near our school. We play......in...... After school, I.....
  Best wishes,

11 Your Language Record

Now complete your *Language Record*.

Time to spare? Choose one of these exercises.

1 Look at Units 1 and 2 and make another word halves exercise (see Exercise 8 of this Unit).
2 Write your school timetable in English and put it in your exercise book.
3 Work with a partner. Play 'I spy' (= see) with the words in the Unit. For example:

| A: I spy with my little eye | B: 'shops'? | B: 'school'? | B: 'some'? |
| a word beginning with 's'. | A: No. | A: No. | A: Yes! |

Language Record

Write or draw the meaning of the words.
Add the missing examples.

Word	Meaning	Example
a break		We have a break at 10 o'clock.
a bus station		The bus station is near the park.
a factory		There is a car factory near the airport.
a farm		My brother has a farm.
a flat		
a hill		My school is on a hill.
a lesson		My favourite lesson is English.
a market		There is a market in the town centre.
a river		There is a river near my house.
a shop		
a subject		We have ten subjects at school.
a timetable		My timetable is in my English book.
a town		
a train station		The train station is in the town centre.
favourite		My favourite day is Friday.
much		I don't know much about Biology.
near		
small		
There are some		There are some shops near here.
go		
know		I know you.
learn		We learn about different things in school.
work		
live		

Choose some more words from this box. Add their meanings and examples.

> a park   a swimming pool   a museum   a library   a guitar   a bus   an office
> north   south   west   east

Your own notes

4 Language focus

1 What's on the map?

Extra practice • WB Ex. 1

1.1 Maps

Have you got a map of your town or country?
What can maps tell you? When can you use a map?

Tell the class your ideas.

1.2 What can maps tell us?

Maps can tell us a lot. They can tell us about the places
we can visit. They can tell us about distances.
They can tell us where things are.

Here is a map of where Anne lives, in Newport.
Look at the map and answer these questions:

There is a castle in square D2. What's in square C4?

How big is the area? (Look at the scale and use a ruler!)

There are many picnic places. How many can you see?

Look at the symbols. What other things are there in the area?

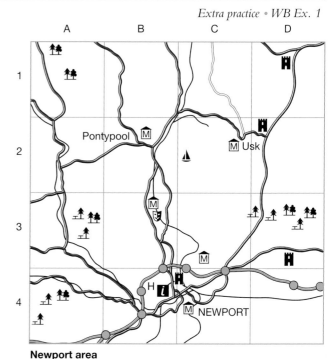

Newport area

Key

Picnic area	🌲	Lake	⛵	Motorway	═══
Hospital	H	Museum	Ⓜ	Main road	━━
Theatre	🛡	Woods	🌲🌲	Railway	──
Information centre	*i*	Castle	🏰		

Scale   0   5   10
km

1.3 Make a map

What places do you know in your area?
Make a list with the class.

Put a four squares by four squares box on
your blackboard. Mark on the roads, rivers,
railways and other important places.
Write the numbers and letters.

Write some sentences to describe your map.

There is a hospital in square A3.

The river goes from square A1 to D4.

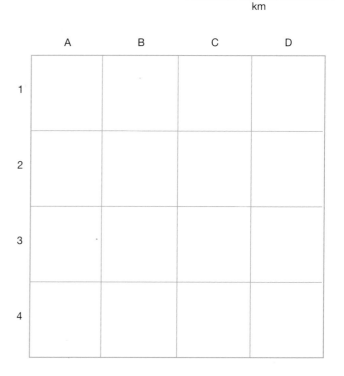

2 Nouns, verbs and adjectives

Parts of speech
Extra practice • WB Ex. 2

2.1 What type of word is it?

Nouns are the names of things. For example: a town   a road   a hospital

Verbs are action words. For example: go   start   walk

Adjectives describe something. For example: big   cold   hot

What do you call nouns, verbs and adjectives in your language? Can you think of examples in your language?

Draw three circles, like this:

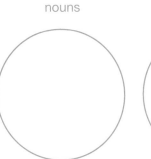 nouns  verbs  adjectives

Now, with your neighbour,
put these words in the correct circle.

bicycle   dance   hot   history   good   country   river
swim   small   go   timetable   beautiful   map

Look at your *Language Records* from Units 2 and 3 and find more words to
put in the circles.

Compare your ideas with the rest of the class.

2.2 Play a game!

If your teacher says a noun, hold up your right hand. If your teacher says a verb,
hold up your left hand. If your teacher says an adjective, shake your head.

3 No, I don't!

*Present simple
positive and negative*
Extra practice • WB Ex. 3
Extra practice •
TB Ws. 4.1, 4.2

3.1 Sentences with 'not'

Look at these examples.

I'm not rich.
We haven't got tigers in our country.
It isn't very hot in our country.
I don't live in England. I don't walk to school.
I don't like football.
My father doesn't work.
I don't know.

How do you say these sentences in your language?

3.2 Describe the negative

How do you make negative sentences?
Write some more negative sentences in the tables.

Subject	+	....	+	....
I You We They		don't		know much about geography.

Subject	+	....	+	....
He She It		doesn't		have lunch at school.

Tell the class your ideas.

3.3 PRACTICE What does your neighbour do?

Find out three things that your neighbour *does* and three things that she or
he *doesn't* do. You can use the verbs below.

Do you swim after school?   *Yes, I do.*
Do you play the piano?   *No, I don't.*

You can use these verbs.
  Do you …

play football   play the piano   like Maths   play the guitar   live near an airport
ride a bicycle   dance   paint   sing   have breakfast before eight o'clock

Tell the class what you know about your neighbour. Remember the 's'.
You can start like this:

  David lives …   He doesn't …

Say it clearly!

Yes, I do.
No, I don't.

Say it clearly!

likes   paints /s/

lives   plays   has
does /z/

3.4 MORE PRACTICE Possible or impossible?

Look at the map of Lanark, where David lives.
Are these sentences possible or impossible?

At the weekend …
1 David goes to the museum in Lanark.
   Possible! There is a museum in Lanark.

2 David goes by train to Rosebank.
   Impossible! David doesn't go by train.
   There isn't a train station in Rosebank.

3 David swims in the sea near Lanark.

4 David swims in the river near Lanark.

5 David rides his bicycle to Carstairs.

6 David visits lots of picnic places near Lanark.

7 David looks at the planes at the airport in Lanark.

8 David walks to the castle.

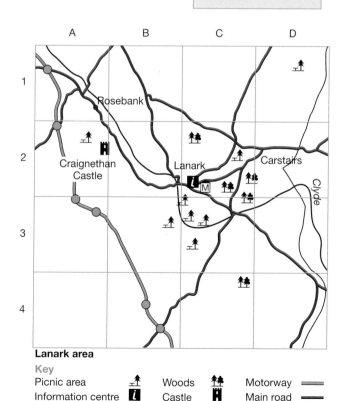

Lanark area
Key
Picnic area ⛺   Woods 🌲   Motorway ═══
Information centre 𝒊   Castle ♜   Main road ▬▬
Museum Ⓜ   River —   Railway ▬▬▬

4 Out and about with English

Going shopping; asking for information
Extra practice • LS Ex. 2

4.1 Pocket money

Do you have pocket money? What do you do with it?

4.2 Mona and Ali go shopping

Listen. What do Mona and Ali want to buy?

MONA: Look, Ali. Here's a cassette of my favourite band. Excuse me, how much is this cassette?

MAN: That's £9.20.

ALI: That's expensive. Let's try another shop.

MONA: Here it is, Ali. Excuse me, can I have that cassette, please?

WOMAN: Here you are. That's £7.40 please.

MONA: Thank you. What do you want, Ali?

ALI: Some computer games and a computer magazine. Let's go to the newsagent's.

MONA: Good. I can get a box of chocolates for Mum there.

ALI: Can I pay for this computer game and magazine, please?

WOMAN: The game is free with the magazine.

ALI: Great!

MONA: Can I have that box of chocolates, please?

WOMAN: Yes, of course. That's £4.75 and £2.50. That's £7.25, please.

ALI: Thanks.

Now you try it. Work with a partner. You are in a shop.
You can change the conversation.

Excuse me, how much is this …?
How much are these …?
Can I have that …, please?
Can I pay for these …, please?

That's …, please.
Here you are.
Yes, of course.

> *Say it clearly!*
>
> | much | this |
> |------|------|
> | these | pay |

£10.50

£12.50

£3.25

50p

25p

£5.50

£10.50

£2.50

£15.25

£2.50

Act out your dialogue for the class.

---

5 Your Language Record

Now complete your *Language Record*.

Time to spare? Choose one of these exercises.

1 Use the *Ideas list* on pages 88–89 to make an exercise for another student.
2 How many subjects can you find in this puzzle? The words go down (↓) and across (→). What word can you make with the letters which are like this?
3 Make a list of some towns, mountains and rivers in your country. Write some sentences about where they are. For example:

> Mount Everest is in the north.
> The River Amazon is in the south.

N
NW	NE
W	E
SW	SE
S

E	N	G	L	I	S	H	S	E	G
H	M	A	T	H	S	A	R	T	E
I	S	D	S	P	O	R	T	Z	O
S	C	G	U	I	D	E	C	F	G
T	I	B	G	M	Y	D	S	Z	R
O	E	K	I	U	T	R	E	D	A
R	N	G	T	S	I	P	N	J	P
Y	C	G	T	I	U	I	J	G	H
M	E	S	I	C	F	R	T	D	Y

Language Record

Your own phrase book! GOING SHOPPING

Add more phrases. Write the meaning in your language.

How much is this? How much are these?	Can I pay for these? ....
Excuse me, can I have … please?	That's ....
I want to buy	Yes, of course. ....
Here you are	

Present simple negative. Complete the table. Write some more examples.

Pronoun	'don't/doesn't'	Verb	Pronoun	'don't/doesn't'	Verb
I	don't	have Maths on Friday.	We		
You	don't	eat lunch at home.	They		
He/She/It					

Present simple. Write some more examples.

Pronoun	Verb	Pronoun	Verb
I	have long hair.	We	go to school by bus.
You	live in a flat.	They	play
He	has long hair.		
She	lives in a flat.		
It			

Learn more about your book!

1 Look at the back of the book

Look at pages 88 to 93.
Complete the list of sections.

Ideas list

....

....

....

What can you do with each section?
Tell the class your ideas.

2 Look at the sections

Where can you find

a a map of Brazil?
b an example of an exercise?
c the words from the book?
d the countries in Africa?
e which words are nouns or verbs?
f something to sing?

3 Look at the Wordlist/Index

In which Units are these words?
Are they nouns, verbs or adjectives?

ride ☐   pull ☐
tall ☐   elephant ☐

In which Unit(s) can you learn about

possessive adjectives? ☐

Present simple questions? ☐

asking for information? ☐

talking about past events? ☐

Topic 5 In the wild

Animals and how they live; curriculum links with Biology, Zoology and Science

1 What is it?

With your neighbour, write the correct letter by each word.

- ☐ a kangaroo
- ☐ a parrot
- ☐ a crocodile
- ☐ a bee
- ☐ an elephant
- ☐ a whale
- ☐ a shark
- ☐ a monkey

Names of animals
Extra practice • WB Ex. 1

2 Buzzz ...

🖭 Listen to some animal sounds. Which animals are they? Write a number beside each picture.

Names of animals
Extra practice • WB Ex. 2

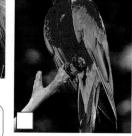

Tell the class your ideas.

> I think it's a horse.

> What's number two?

> I don't think so. I think it's a cow.

3 Mammals, reptiles, insects, birds and fish

Types of animals

There are many types of animals. Here are some definitions.
Match the two halves of the definitions.

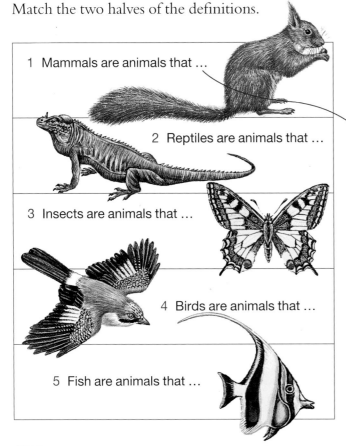

1 Mammals are animals that ...	a ... lay eggs. Many of them can fly. Their blood is warm.
2 Reptiles are animals that ...	b ... give milk to their babies. They have warm blood.
3 Insects are animals that ...	c ... have cold blood. They all lay eggs and their skin is thick.
4 Birds are animals that ...	d ... live in water. Their blood is cold.
5 Fish are animals that ...	e ... have six legs. Most of them have wings and can fly.

Compare answers with your neighbour
and then listen to the cassette to check them.

Look at the animals in Exercises 1 and 2. Are they mammals, reptiles,
insects, birds or fish? Tell the class what you think.

4 What are we?

People are also a type of animal. Are these sentences true (√) or false (✗)?

☐ We give milk to our babies.   ☐ We lay eggs.
☐ We live in water.   ☐ Our blood is warm.
☐ Our skin is thick.   ☐ We have six legs.

What type of animal are we?

5 Sing a song! Wimoweh

Listen to 'Wimoweh' and sing it with your class.
The words are on page 90.

6 How do they live?

Here is some more information about animals.

Look through the information and find an animal that

a sleeps for eight hours at night.
b lives for twenty years.
c eats insects and fruit.
d eats grass and sleeps for five hours.

Information about animals

giraffe

How many hours do they sleep?

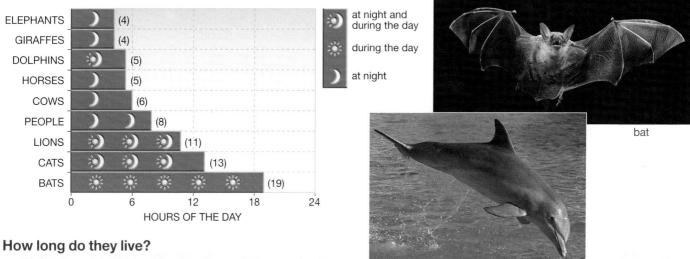

ELEPHANTS (4)
GIRAFFES (4)
DOLPHINS (5)
HORSES (5)
COWS (6)
PEOPLE (8)
LIONS (11)
CATS (13)
BATS (19)

0   6   12   18   24
HOURS OF THE DAY

at night and during the day
during the day
at night

bat

dolphin

How long do they live?

people	elephants	dolphins	horses	cows	lions	giraffes	cats	bats
75 years	60 years	50 years	25 years	20 years	20 years	20 years	15 years	5 years

What do they eat?

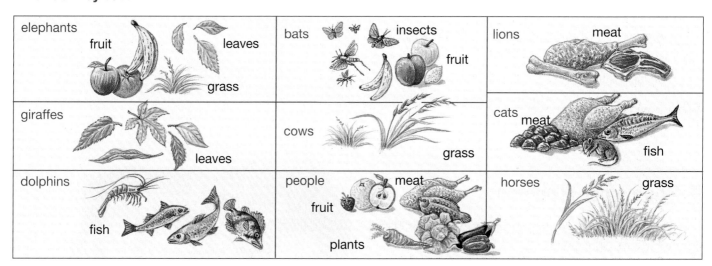

elephants — fruit, leaves, grass

giraffes — leaves

dolphins — fish

bats — insects, fruit

cows — grass

people — fruit, meat, plants

lions — meat

cats — meat, fish

horses — grass

7 Ask about the animals

Extra practice • LS Ex. 1–2

Now, in pairs, ask each other about the animals.

What do elephants eat? *They eat fruit, leaves and grass.*

How long do lions live? *They live for 20 years.*

How many hours do cats sleep? *They sleep for 13 hours.*

> **Say it clearly!**
>
> elephants /s/
> cows /z/
> horses /ɪz/

8 Which animal is it?

Listening

Listen to part of a radio programme about animals.
Which animal are they talking about?

9 Your own radio programme

Speaking

Extra practice • WB Ex. 3

Imagine you are a famous explorer. You have discovered a very
strange animal. Draw a picture of the animal and complete the report.
Give the animal a name.

ANIMAL REPORT

Name of animal:

What does it look like?
It has ...

What does it eat?

How many hours does it sleep?

Where does it live?

How long does it live?

Now imagine that you are on the radio.
With your neighbour, prepare a radio
interview. You can use the questions to help
you. Act out your interview for the class.

10 Decide …

You can work by yourself, with a partner or in a small group.
Choose an exercise.

Exercise 10.1 practises asking questions.
Exercise 10.2 practises writing.

Or you can do **something else**. Talk to your teacher and decide what to do.
(You can use the *Ideas list* on pages 88–89 to make an exercise.)

10.1 A game about some animals   *Asking questions*

One person thinks of an animal. The other people ask questions to find out the
name of the animal. The person can only say 'Yes, it is/does' or
'No, it isn't/doesn't'. Like this:

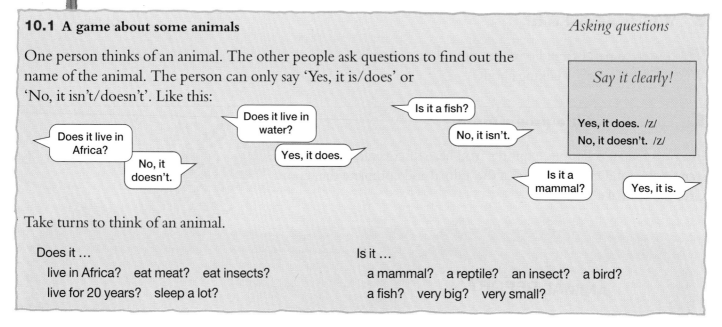

Take turns to think of an animal.

Does it …	Is it …
live in Africa? eat meat? eat insects?	a mammal? a reptile? an insect? a bird?
live for 20 years? sleep a lot?	a fish? very big? very small?

10.2 Write about some animals

Read this description. Which animal is it about?

Now write about three more animals.
Give your descriptions to some other students.
Can they guess which animals they are?

> This animal is a mammal
> and lives in Africa. It sleeps
> four hours a day and it
> doesn't eat meat. It lives
> for about 20 years.

11 Your Language Record

Now complete your *Language Record*.

Time to spare? Choose one of these exercises.

1 Choose an exercise from your class *Exercise Box* or use the *Ideas list* on pages 88–89
  to make an exercise for your class *Exercise Box*.
2 Think of an animal and write a dialogue like the one in Exercise 10.1. Write the
  name of the animal on the back. Give it to another student to read and guess.
3 Imagine … You are on another planet. You can see a strange animal. What is it?
  Draw a picture and write a description. (See Exercise 9.)

Language Record

Write or draw the meaning of the words.
Add the missing examples.

Word	Meaning	Example
a mammal		A whale is a mammal.
a bird		There is a bird in the tree.
a fish, fish		Do you like fish?
a baby, babies		Mammals give their babies milk.
a leg		Insects have six legs.
an insect		Bees are insects.
an egg		Birds lay eggs.
milk		Baby whales drink milk.
water		Fish live in water.
meat		
blood		Reptiles have cold blood.
people		
fruit		
warm		Our blood is warm.
cold		It is very cold today.
(to) sleep		Bats sleep during the day.
at night		Elephants sleep at night.
during the day		Bats sleep during the day.
How long …?		
What …?		
When …?		
How many …?		

Choose some more words from this box. Add their meanings and examples.

> a kangaroo   a parrot   a whale   a crocodile   a shark   a bee   a monkey   a cow
>
> a sheep   a dolphin   a lion   a giraffe   a bat   to fly   to lay   skin   thick   a wing

Your own notes

6 Language focus

1 Some more animals

Discussion

Extra practice • WB Ex. 1

Here are some more animals.
What do you know about them?
Tell the class your ideas.

Where do they live?

> in trees   in rivers
> underground   by the sea ...

What do they eat?

> insects   plants
> mammals   fish ...

Where in the world do they live?

> in Asia   Africa   Europe
> Antarctica   India   Australia
> North America   South America

NATURE MONTHLY

The Wonderful World of Animals

A panda ➤

A hippopotamus
▼

▼ A tarantula

A humming bird ▲

54

55

2 Which animal is it?

Listening

Anne and her friend Pat are looking at the magazine from
Exercise 1. Listen. Which animal are they talking about?

ANNE: Gosh! How beautiful!
PAT: Yes, it is.
ANNE: Where do they live?
PAT: In trees, of course.
ANNE: I know that! I mean where
    in the world do they live?
PAT: Oh sorry. Well, they live in
    North America and South America.
    Countries like Mexico and Brazil.
ANNE: How do they fly like that?
PAT: Well, they move their wings very fast.
    They drink nectar from flowers.
ANNE: Oh. You're clever. How do you
    know all this?
PAT: I've got this magazine at home!
ANNE: Oh!

3 Asking questions

Present simple questions

Extra practice • WB Ex. 2, 4
Extra practice • LS Ex. 2
Extra practice • TB Ws. 6.2

3.1 Types of questions

In Units 3 and 4, there were questions with the verb 'be' ('am/is/are'). Like this:

Where is the airport?   Where are the factories?

In this Unit and Unit 5, there are questions with 'do' or 'does'. Like this:

What does it eat?   Do insects sleep?   How long do lions live?

Look at Units 1–5 again. Find some more questions with 'do' or 'does'. Write down five or six examples. Read out some questions to your class and put some on the board. What do they mean in your language?

3.2 Describe the questions

Look at your examples and complete the description in the table. Make notes about questions in the Present simple.

Tell the class about your ideas.
Where is the verb?
Where is the subject?

Present simple questions
Do | +......................
         | | +......................
Does | +......................
Notes

3.3 SOME MORE PRACTICE

Work with a partner and do Exercises A, B and C.

A Which piece goes where? Choose the correct piece 1–8 for each space A–H.

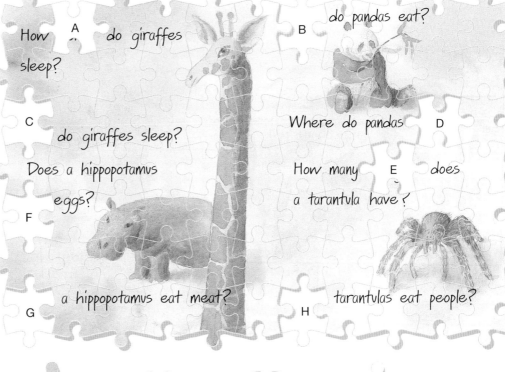

How   A ..   do giraffes sleep?

B   do pandas eat?

C   do giraffes sleep?

Does a hippopotamus   F   eggs?

Where do pandas   D

How many   E   does a tarantula have?

a hippopotamus eat meat?   G

H   tarantulas eat people?

1 lay
2 live?
3 Does
4 When
5 Do
6 long
7 legs
8 What

B Write the questions next to the right answer.

How long do giraffes sleep?   They sleep about four hours a day.

....   They sleep at night.

....   They eat bamboo.

....   They live in China.

....   No, it doesn't. It eats grass.

....   No! It's a mammal.

....   It has eight legs.

....   No, they don't. But they bite people!

C Look back at Unit 5, Exercise 6 and write four more questions about animals. Ask some other students to write their answers. Put your questions in your class *Exercise Box.* You can use these words:

How long …?   How many …?   What …?   Where …?
When …?   Do …?   Does …?

How long do dolphins sleep?

Dolphins sleep for five hours.

What type of animals have cold blood?

Reptiles have cold blood.

4 **'my, your, his, her' …**

4.1 What do you say?

How do you say these sentences in your language?

Possessive adjectives
Extra practice • WB Ex. 3
Extra practice •
TB Ws. 6.2

Our skin is thick.

Snakes are reptiles, too. **Their** blood is cold.

You move **your** wings very fast.

A cow gives milk to **its** babies.

Words like 'their', 'its', 'your', and 'our' are called *possessive adjectives.* Other possessives are 'my', 'his' and 'her'. In English, there are different possessive adjectives for each person.

4.2 Complete the box

Put the correct possessive adjective in this box. Add the examples that are
missing and the meaning in your language.

Subject	Possessive	Meaning	Example
I	my	....	Where is my parrot?
you (singular)	....	....	....
he	....	....	That's his cow.
she	....	....	Her horse is very old.
it	....	....	....
we	....	....	....
you (plural)	....	....	What's your name?
they	....	....	....

You can also make possessives with names of people or things:

Pat's book   Anne's house   the boy's hair

4.3 PRACTICE using possessive adjectives

Work in pairs. Take turns to start.

A: *Whose dog is this?*

B: *It's his dog.*

5 Out and about with English

Making new friends: asking for information and inviting

5.1 Mona makes a new friend

There is a new girl in Mona's school. What questions can Mona ask her?
Make a list.

What's …?   Do you have …?   Do you like …?   Where …?

5.2 Mona's questions

Listen. How many of your questions does Mona ask?

MONA: Hello. What's your name?
SOPHIE: Sophie. What's your name?
MONA: Mona. Do you want a sweet?
SOPHIE: Thanks.
MONA: Do you want to play volleyball?
SOPHIE: I don't know how to play.
MONA: It's easy. I can show you.
SOPHIE: OK. Let's go.
MONA: Where do you live?
SOPHIE: In Prospect Street.

MONA: That's near my house. Do you want to come to my house tomorrow?
SOPHIE: I don't know. I can ask my dad.
MONA: All right. What's your telephone number?
SOPHIE: We haven't got a telephone. I can ask him after school.
MONA: OK.

5.3 PRACTICE

Now you try it. Work with a partner. You can change Mona and Sophie's dialogue.

Do you want   a sweet?

a piece of chewing gum?

a biscuit?

Do you want to play   volleyball?

football?

basketball?

Where do you live?   In …
What's your telephone number?   It's …
I can ring you later.

Act out your dialogue for the class.

6   Your Language Record

Now complete your *Language Record*.

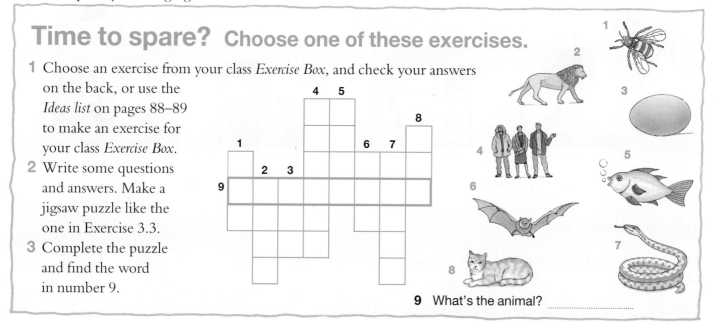

Time to spare? Choose one of these exercises.

1 Choose an exercise from your class *Exercise Box*, and check your answers on the back, or use the *Ideas list* on pages 88–89 to make an exercise for your class *Exercise Box*.
2 Write some questions and answers. Make a jigsaw puzzle like the one in Exercise 3.3.
3 Complete the puzzle and find the word in number 9.

9 What's the animal? ....

Language Record

Your own phrase book! MAKING NEW FRIENDS
Add more phrases. Write the meaning in your language.

Do you want …? .... Let's go. ....
Do you want to play …? .... Where do you live? ....
I don't know how to. .... What's your telephone number? ....
....
....
....

Write some examples in the table.

	'do/does'	Subject	Verb
How many legs	do	insects	have?
Where	does	that cat	live?
When			
What			

Fill in the possessive.

I → my   we → ....
you → ....   you → ....
he → ....   they → ....
she → ....
it → ....

Your own notes

....
....
....

Revision Box Numbers

Revise the numbers and then play bingo!

20 twenty   30 thirty   40 forty   50 fifty   60 sixty   70 seventy   80 eighty   90 ninety   100 a hundred

Write down how you say these numbers.

13 *thirteen* .... 46 .... 88 ....

17 .... 54 *fifty-four* .... 94 ....

23 *twenty-three* .... 65 .... 111 *a hundred and eleven*

30 *thirty* .... 70 .... 120 ....

Choose a board. Listen to the numbers and put a cross if you have the numbers. Shout BINGO! when you have crosses on all your numbers.

Board 1			
23	14	26	17
54	29	31	

Board 2			
55	5	13	18
24	30	11	

Board 3			
28	100	88	101
40	12	70	

Board 4			
67	81	61	21
15	7	38	

Board 5			
4	60	99	90
1	42	3	

Board 6			
2	92	19	16
9	10	45	

Elements in 'good' food;
curriculum links with
Health Education

Theme D The way we live

7 Topic Food matters

1 The foods you like *Discussion*

What is your favourite food? Which foods don't you like? Which foods do you think are good for you? Why? Which foods do you think are bad for you? Why?

2 The food you eat

Work by yourself. Write down your answers to the questionnaire. Compare your answers with your neighbour and other students in your class.

3 How do you start the day?

What do you have for breakfast?
Tell your neighbour.

For breakfast, I have …

some cereal

an egg

some juice

a roll

some milk

some hot chocolate

some cheese

a pastry

some fruit

some bread

WHAT DO YOU EAT?

1 How many meals do you eat every day?
- ❏ a three or more
- ❏ b two
- ❏ c one

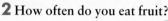

2 How often do you eat fruit?
- ❏ a three times a day
- ❏ b once or twice a day
- ❏ c three or four times a week (or less)

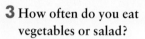

3 How often do you eat vegetables or salad?
- ❏ a three times a day
- ❏ b once or twice a day
- ❏ c three or four times a week (or less)

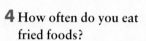

4 How often do you eat fried foods?
- ❏ a almost every day
- ❏ b three or four times a week
- ❏ c once or twice a week (or less)

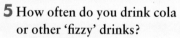

5 How often do you drink cola or other 'fizzy' drinks?
- ❏ a almost every day
- ❏ b three or four times a week
- ❏ c once or twice a week (or less)

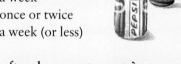

6 How often do you eat sweets?
- ❏ a almost every day
- ❏ b three or four times a week
- ❏ c once or twice a week (or less)

4 Some more things to eat

Do you know the names of these foods? Label the pictures.

Names of foods
Extra practice • WB Ex. 1
Extra practice • LS Ex. 2

bread   butter
sugar   meat
fish   cheese
milk   vegetables
eggs   fruit
rice   pasta
potatoes

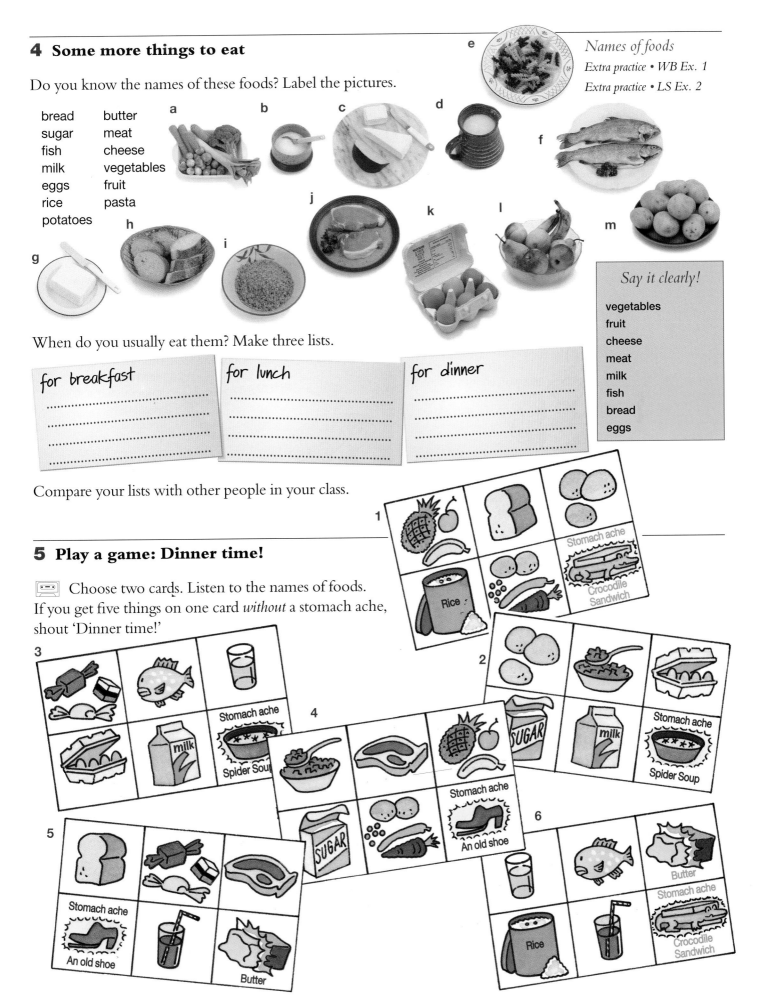

Say it clearly!

vegetables
fruit
cheese
meat
milk
fish
bread
eggs

When do you usually eat them? Make three lists.

for breakfast

....
....
....
....

for lunch

....
....
....
....

for dinner

....
....
....
....

Compare your lists with other people in your class.

5 Play a game: Dinner time!

Choose two cards. Listen to the names of foods.
If you get five things on one card *without* a stomach ache,
shout 'Dinner time!'

6 Eat well, stay healthy!

Read about the foods we eat. Do *you* eat all of
the 'seven important things'?

Reading
Extra practice • WB Ex. 2–3
Extra practice • LS Ex. 1

EAT WELL
stay healthy

Good food has seven important things.

CARBOHYDRATES give you energy.
There are carbohydrates in bread,
sugar, potatoes, pasta and rice.

FATS make you strong and
give you energy. There are
fats in meat, butter
and cheese and oil.

VITAMINS are important
for your eyes, your skin, your
bones, your hair and for other
parts of your body. There are
13 types of vitamins (A, B, C,
and so on). There are vitamins
in many types of food.

PROTEIN helps you to grow and gives
you energy. There is protein in meat,
fish and milk.

WATER is important for
your blood. It also
cleans your body from
the inside. Drink lots
of water every day!

MINERALS make your bones and teeth strong. There are
different types of
minerals in milk,
vegetables, eggs,
meat, cereals and
many other foods.

FIBRE cleans
the inside of
your body.
There is fibre
in nuts, beans
and
cereals.

DANGER!
HIGH IN CARBOHYDRATES!
HIGH IN SUGAR AND SALT!
HIGH IN FATS!
LOW IN FIBRE!
LOW IN VITAMINS!

You can hear the article on the cassette.

7 In the supermarket

Comprehension

Look at this picture. Can you write the correct name on the signs?

What is in these baskets? Carbohydrates, fats, fibre, protein or minerals?

1   2   3   4

Which basket do you think is the best basket?

I think it is basket number … because it has some …   *It doesn't have any … in it.*

8   Decide …

You can work by yourself, with a partner or in a small group.
Choose an exercise.

Exercise 8.1 is about vocabulary.
Exercise 8.2 gives you writing practice about meals.

Or you can do **something else**. Talk to your teacher and decide
what to do. (You can use the *Ideas list* on pages 88–89 to make
an exercise.)

8.1   A puzzle   *Vocabulary*

Can you complete the puzzle? What word do the clues spell?

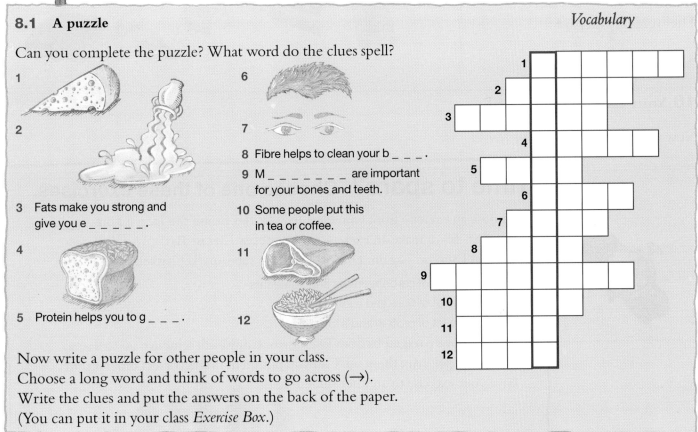

8 Fibre helps to clean your b _ _ _ .

9 M _ _ _ _ _ _ _ are important
for your bones and teeth.

3 Fats make you strong and
give you e _ _ _ _ _ .

10 Some people put this
in tea or coffee.

5 Protein helps you to g _ _ _ .

Now write a puzzle for other people in your class.
Choose a long word and think of words to go across (→).
Write the clues and put the answers on the back of the paper.
(You can put it in your class *Exercise Box*.)

8.2 Write a menu

Read the article in Exercise 6 again. Write a healthy menu for a day that has all of the seven important things. Write a list for each meal.

9 Sing a song! I love chocolate

Listen to 'I love chocolate' and sing it with your class. The words are on page 91.

10 Your Language Record

Now complete your *Language Record*.

Time to spare? Choose one of these exercises.

1 Choose an exercise from your class *Exercise Box* or use the *Ideas list* on pages 88–89 to make an exercise for your class *Exercise Box*.

2 Look at Exercise 7 again. Draw three more supermarket baskets:

- one with a lot of carbohydrates and some fats
- one with a lot of fibre and a lot of minerals
- one with a lot of protein and a lot of fats

3 Choose three paragraphs from Exercise 6. Copy each sentence on to a small piece of paper. Mix them up. Can you put them in the correct order again? Give your exercise to another student to do.

Language Record

Write or draw the meaning of the words.
Add the missing examples.

Word	Meaning	Example
a meal		How many meals do you eat a day?
a sweet		Do you want a sweet?
a vegetable		Do you like vegetables?
a body		Fats make your body strong.
bread		Bread has a lot of fibre in it.
butter		
sugar		Do you have sugar in tea or coffee?
meat		Do you eat meat?
breakfast		What time do you have breakfast?
lunch		
dinner		When do you have dinner?
important		
less		I eat sweets less than once a week.
often		How often do you eat fruit?
give		Carbohydrates give you energy.
make		Fats make you strong.
clean		
help		

Choose four more words. Write some examples and the meaning.

> cheese   an egg   fruit   rice   pasta   a potato   oil   eyes   skin
> bones   teeth   hair   healthy   different   milk   once   twice   three times

Your own notes

8 Language focus

1 Can you cook?

Discussion

Do you like cooking? Do you know any recipes? Tell the class.

2 What are they making?

Listening

Extra practice • WB Ex. 1

Look at the recipes and listen.

Pat and Anne want to make something. What is it?
Can they make it? What *can* they make?

PANCAKES

You need:
2 cups of flour
1 cup of milk
1 cup of water
1 egg

SHORTBREAD BISCUITS

You need:
350g of flour
225g of butter
100g of sugar
some salt

PAT: OK. Let's see. What do we need?
        Have we got any flour?
ANNE: Yes. We've got lots of flour. Here.
PAT: Good. We need some butter, too.
        Have we got any butter?
ANNE: Some butter ... butter ...
        We've got a lot of milk, but butter ...
        Ah, yes. Here we are.
PAT: Excellent.
ANNE: We've got six eggs. Do you want them?
PAT: Er ... no. We don't need any eggs. Sugar?
ANNE: Sugar ... sugar ... sugar. No!
        We haven't got any sugar.
PAT: Oh no! I know! We can make ...

3 What do we have?

'some' and 'any'

Extra practice • WB Ex. 2

Extra practice • TB Ws. 8.1

3.1 What do you say?

How do you say these sentences in your language?

We have some eggs.
We don't have any butter.
Do you have any sugar?

What do 'some' and 'any' mean in your language?

3.2 A grammar puzzle

When do you say 'some'? When do you say 'any'?

Look at the sentences below.
With your neighbour, work out a rule.

You say 'some' when...   *You say 'any' when...*

We need some butter.
For breakfast, I have some bread and milk.
We have some eggs.

Do we have any flour?
Do we have any butter?
Do we need any eggs?

We don't need any eggs.
We don't have any sugar.
I don't have any money.

Say it clearly!

some butter
some bread
any sugar
any eggs

Compare your rule with others in your class.
Then compare it with the rule that your teacher has.

3.3 PRACTICE with 'some' and 'any'

First label the things in this picture.

bread cheese butter eggs
sugar fish potatoes milk

Now, test your memory. Look at
the picture for a few moments.
Try to remember what is in it.
Then close your book.

Your teacher will say the names of some foods. Write a sentence about each one. For example:

 apples   *There aren't any apples in the picture.*

eggs   *There are some eggs in the picture.*

Check the picture to see if you are right.

4 'them, it, her, him' ...

Object pronouns
Extra practice • WB Ex. 3
Extra practice • TB Ws. 8.2

4.1 What do you say?

How do you say these sentences in your language?

Vitamins are important. You need (them)!   That's Peter. Do you know (him)?
This is my new bike. Do you like (it)?   There's Sujita. Can you see (her)?

Words like 'them', 'it', 'him' and 'her' are called *object pronouns*. Draw a line to show
what each one talks about.

Vitamins are important. You need (them)!

4.2 PRACTICE

Work with your neighbour. Ask each other about the pictures.

Do you like football?
I don't mind it.
I think it's OK.

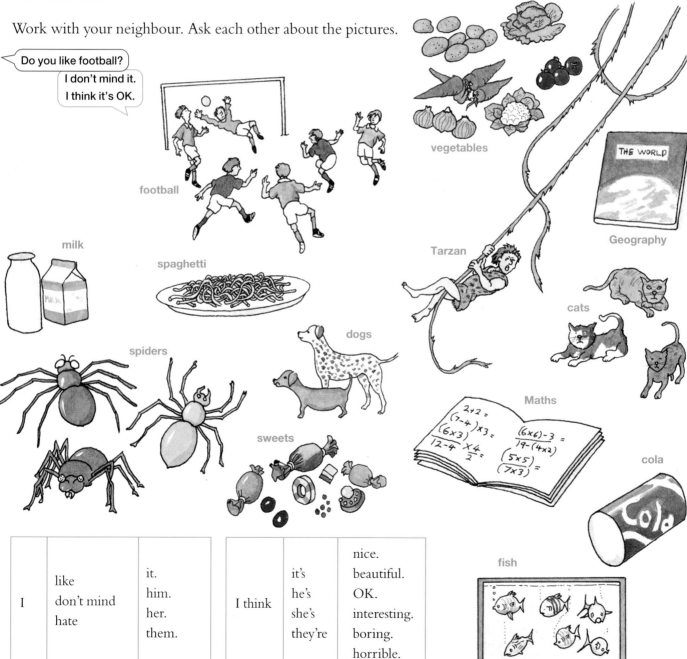

vegetables

THE WORLD

Geography

football

milk

spaghetti

Tarzan

cats

dogs

spiders

Maths

cola

sweets

fish

I	like don't mind hate	it. him. her. them.		I think	it's he's she's they're	nice. beautiful. OK. interesting. boring. horrible.

5 Out and about with English

Talking about likes and dislikes

Extra practice • LS Ex. 2

5.1 Sophie visits Mona's house

Sophie is in Mona's house.
Look at the picture. What do
you think they are talking about?

5.2 Are you right?

Listen. Are you right?

MONA: Well. This is my bedroom.
SOPHIE: Oh … er, it's very nice.
MONA: No, it's not! It's terrible!
SOPHIE: Well, yes …
MONA: But I like it. I've got a new CD.
The Mash Boys. Do you like them?
SOPHIE: The Mash Boys. I don't know them.
MONA: What! Listen. What do you think?
SOPHIE: Well, it's not my favourite music.
I like Sleeping Giants.

MONA: Oh, yeah. They're nice.
Here. Listen to this.
Do you like it?
SOPHIE: Pardon?
MONA: Do you like it?
SOPHIE: Well, it's OK.
MONA: Pardon?
SOPHIE: No, I don't like it.
MONA: Oh, OK.

Do you like Mona's music?

5.3 PRACTICE

Now you try it. Work with a partner.
Talk about your friend's things.
You can change Mona and Sophie's dialogue.

bedroom   *pet cat*   *pet dog*

These are my   *games*   *books*   *cassettes*

Do you like it/them?
I think it's/they're   nice
*   terrible   beautiful*
*   interesting   boring   horrible …*

Do you have any …?

Act out your dialogue for the class.

Something to make at home

You can make pancakes and shortbread at home.

IMPORTANT!
Do this with an adult

Pancakes

You need:

2 cups of flour   1 cup of water
1 cup of milk   1 egg

1. Mix everything together.
2. Put some of the liquid into a frying pan.
3. Cook the pancakes on both sides.
4. Delicious with lemon and sugar!

Shortbread biscuits

You need:

350g of flour   100g of sugar
225g of butter   some salt

1. Mix everything together.
2. Put into a cooking tin.
3. Put it into the oven at 170°C for one hour.
4. Cut it into pieces. Delicious with a glass of milk!

---

6   Your Language Record

Now complete your *Language Record*.

Time to spare?   Choose one of these exercises.

1 Choose an exercise from your class *Exercise Box* and check your answers on the back, or use the *Ideas list* on pages 88–89 to make an exercise for your class *Exercise Box*.

2 Match the parts of the words with the pictures.

br
but
chee
e
mil
po
su

ter
tatoes
se
k
ggs
gar
ead

3 Write three sentences that are true and three sentences that are false about your house or bedroom. Ask another student to guess which sentences are false.

There are three bedrooms in my house. True!
There aren't any televisions in my house. False!

Language Record

Your own phrase book! LIKES AND DISLIKES

Add more phrases. Write the meaning in your language.

Do you like ...?	....
I like it. ·	....
I don't mind it.	....
I don't like it.	....
I think it's nice/beautiful/OK/ interesting/boring/horrible.	....

'Some' and 'any': a rule.   Write more examples (look at the picture in Exercise 3.3).

You use 'some' for positive sentences.
We have some eggs.
....
....
....

You use 'any' for questions and negatives.
We don't have any apples.
....

Do we have any butter?

Complete the table and the examples.

Subject	Object	Example
I	me	Can you tell me the time?
you (singular)	....	My dog likes you.
he	....	Do they know ....?
she		Can you see ....?

Subject	Object	Example
it	it	Do you have ....?
we	us	Good food is important for ....
you (plural)	....	I have some plants for you.
they	them	We need ....!

Revision Box Can

1 'Can' has many meanings. You can use it to:

say what you can do
I can swim very well

ask to do something
Can I open the window?

say if something is possible
Can you eat metal?

ask if you can do something
Can I go home, now?

2 Say what you can do.

Talk to your neighbour. Find out: four things that both of you can do.
four things that both of you can't do.

Can you speak French?   No!
Can you play football?   Yes!

Tell the class.

We can play football, run very well, sing and swim.
We can't speak French, cook, play tennis or drive a car.

3 Say if something is possible.

Play a game. Your teacher will give one person something in a bag.
Only that person can see it. The other students can ask questions:
Guess what it is!

Can you eat it? Can you find it in a bedroom?
Can you write with it? Can you open it?
Can you find it in this classroom?

9 Topic Into space

Space, stars and planets; curriculum links with Science and Geography

1 The planets

Music and discussion

Listen to part of Holst's *The Planets Suite*. While you are listening, look at the pictures in this Unit.

Do you like the music? What things do you imagine when you hear it? What do other students in your class think?

2 Our place in space

Look at the pictures again and read about space.
While you are reading, make some notes.
Like this:

Things I knew already
　　　　The Earth is 75% water.
Things I didn't know
　　　　The sky is history.
Things I don't understand
　　　　　　expand?
　　　　　　gravity?

When you are ready, compare your notes with your neighbour. Help each other to understand the text.

1 OUR SOLAR SYSTEM

There are nine planets in our solar system. The smallest planet is Pluto. It is also the coldest because it is a long way from the sun. The Earth goes around the sun in $365\frac{1}{4}$ days (one year) but Pluto takes 248 years!

2 THE UNIVERSE IS EXPANDING!

Astronomers know that the universe is expanding. The stars are moving away from each other. They are not sure why this is happening. Our sun is a star, too. We are moving with the sun.

3 THE SKY IS HISTORY!

It takes a long time for light from the stars to come to Earth. From the nearest star to Earth, it takes about $4\frac{1}{2}$ years. From other stars, light can take millions of years to come to us! In the sky, we can see how the stars WERE many years ago, not how they are NOW.

What do you think? Are we alone in the universe?
Is there life on other planets?

4 THE EARTH FROM SPACE

From space, you can see that 75% of the Earth is water. There is life on Earth because it is not too hot or too cold and there is air. Is there life on other planets? Astronomers don't think so but it is possible that there are more planets in the universe. Perhaps there is life there.

3 What do you know about the moon?

What do you know about the moon?
With your class, brainstorm your ideas.

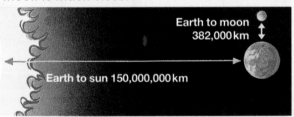

4 The moon, our nearest neighbour

Extra practice • WB Ex. 1–2
Extra practice • LS Ex. 1

Read about the moon.
Are there any points you can add to your ideas from Exercise 3?

THE MOON, OUR NEAREST NEIGHBOUR

Our closest neighbour is the moon. In the sky, the moon and the sun are the same size because the moon is much closer!

Earth to moon 382,000 km

Earth to sun 150,000,000 km

The moon is very different from Earth. Gravity on the moon is six times weaker than on Earth. There isn't any air. During the day, it is very, very hot but at night it is very, very cold. Nothing can live on the moon.

The moon makes the tides – the changes in the level of the sea. The moon and the sun together pull the water. In some parts of the world the difference between 'high tide' (when the water is very close to the land) and 'low tide' (when the water is far away from the land) is very big. This is very important for ships.

You can listen to the text on the cassette.

5 Sing a song! Space

Listen to 'Space' and sing it with your class.
The words are on page 91.

6 The first people on the moon

Listening; Present continuous

6.1 On the moon

In 1969, Neil Armstrong and Buzz Aldrin went to the moon in
the Apollo XI rocket. Look at the pictures and listen to what the
astronauts and the television presenter said at the time.

◀ He's getting on the ladder.

He's going down ▼ the ladder.

▲ The ship is landing on the moon.

▲ He's opening the door.

He's putting his foot on the moon. ▶

6.2 On television

What do you think the
television presenter said
for these pictures?
Write a sentence for each one.

Compare your work with
your neighbour and check
with the rest of the class.

put up a flag

collect rocks

drive a moon-car

go up the ladder

close the door

leave the moon

7 Decide ...

Extra practice • WB Ex. 3–4

You can work by yourself, with a partner or in a small group. Choose an exercise.

Exercise 7.1 gives you speaking practice in an interview with Neil Armstrong.
Exercise 7.2 gives you writing practice about a postcard from the moon.

Or you can do **something else**. Talk to your teacher and decide what to do.
(You can use the *Ideas list* on pages 88–89 to make an exercise.)

7.1 Act out a conversation with Neil Armstrong

Speaking

Imagine that you are in the Space Control Centre.
You are talking to Neil Armstrong on the moon.
What questions can you ask him? What does he answer?
Write down your questions and his answers. For example:

When you are ready, act out your conversation for the class.

7.2 Postcard from the moon

Writing

Imagine that you are on the moon.
Write a postcard to your family and
friends back on Earth! Tell them
about the moon, what you can see
and what you are doing.

POST CARD

Dear everybody at home

Here we are on the moon!
It's very _____

We can see _____

At the moment we are
_____

Best Wishes _____

How does a rocket work?

From Physics, we know that for every action there is an opposite reaction. Modern rockets have liquid fuel and something to help it burn (an oxidizer). This makes a powerful exhaust through the back of the rocket and pushes the rocket up.

... you can try it at home!

Have a race with your friends!

1 Tie a long piece of string to a door handle.

2 Blow up a balloon and stick a drinking straw on it.

3 Put the string through the straw.

4 Hold the string tight and let go of the balloon.

Get more balloons and string and have a race with your friends.

8 Your Language Record

Now complete your *Language Record*.

Time to spare? Choose one of these exercises.

1 Choose an exercise from your class *Exercise Box* or use the *Ideas list* on pages 88–89 to make an exercise for the *Exercise Box*.

2 Neil Armstrong is in the space ship, on the way to the moon. He is talking to the Space Control Centre. Write his answers to these questions:

What can you see? Can you see the moon? What does it look like?
What are you doing? What is Buzz Aldrin doing?

3 Fill in the missing words.

Mercury is a ....   Our planet is called ....
The sun is at the centre of our ....   The sun is a ....
.... are changes in the level of the sea.
You are lighter on the moon because the .... is weaker.
Nothing lives on the moon because there isn't any ....

Language Record

Write or draw the meaning of the words. Add the missing examples.

Word	Meaning	Example
a neighbour		
a picture		
a ship		
alone		Are you alone?
light (adj.)		On the moon, you are much lighter.
light (n.)		The sun gives us light.
same		
so		I don't have any money so I can't go to the film.
strong		The gravity on Earth is stronger than on the moon.
weak		Gravity on the moon is very weak.
sure		I'm not sure.
collect		He's collecting rocks.
expand		The universe is expanding.
go down		He's going down the ladder.
happen		What is happening?
leave		The spaceship is leaving.
move		
pull		Pull the door to open it.
put		He's putting his foot on the moon.
take		Can I take a sweet?
take		It takes many years for light to come from the stars.

Choose four more words. Write some examples and the meaning.

gravity   air   life   perhaps   a star   size   nearer   the tide

Your own notes

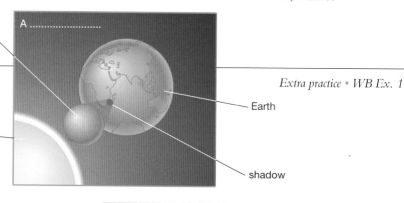

moon

sun

Earth

shadow

A ....

1 Night in the day

Extra practice • WB Ex. 1

Are you afraid of the dark? Sometimes
it is dark during the day …

> If the moon goes between the Earth and
> the sun, we have an *eclipse of the sun.*
> The moon stops the light from the sun
> and we have night in the day.

> If the Earth goes between the moon and
> the sun, we have an *eclipse of the moon.*
> The moon goes into the shadow and it
> disappears for a few minutes.

Which diagram shows an eclipse of the sun? Which
diagram shows an eclipse of the moon? Label the diagrams.

Have you seen an eclipse of the moon or an eclipse of the sun?

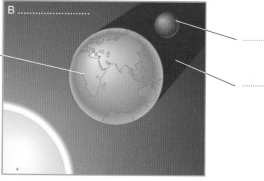

B ....

2 Mexico, 1992

Listening

In 1992 in Yucatán, Mexico, there was a
very clear eclipse. Listen to what the American
television presenter said at the time.

Is she talking about an eclipse of the sun or an
eclipse of the moon? Can you write the correct
time for numbers 1–7 under the picture?

Yucatán, Mexico

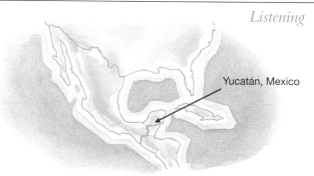

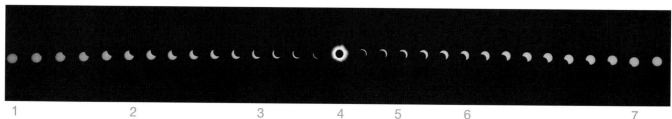

1   2   3   4   5   6   7

YOU can see an eclipse of the sun!

DANGER!
Never look directly at the sun.

Date	Type of eclipse	Where to see it
Aug 11, 1999	Total	Europe, North America, Arabia
July 1, 2000	Partial	South America
Dec 25, 2000	Partial	North America
June 21, 2001	Total	Africa

Date	Type of eclipse	Where to see it
Dec 4, 2002	Total	South Africa, Australia
Nov 23, 2003	Total	
Apr 8, 2005	Mixed	
Mar 29, 2006	Total	

3 What are they doing?

Present continuous
Extra practice • WB Ex. 2
Extra practice • TB Ws. 10.1

3.1 What differences do you notice?

In Units 3–8, you saw *Present simple* sentences like these:

> Giraffes live in Africa. They sleep four hours a day and they don't eat meat.
> They live for about 20 years.

In this Unit and Unit 9, you saw *Present continuous* sentences, like these.

From Unit 9:

He's opening the door.　　He's getting on the ladder.

From Unit 10:

 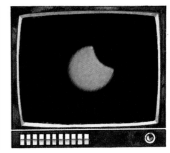

We are all waiting for the eclipse.　　The eclipse is starting.

How do you say these sentences in your language?

What differences do you notice between the Present simple verbs and the Present continuous verbs?

When do you think we use 'be + –ing'? Tell the class your ideas.

3.2 How to form the Present continuous

Can you complete this table?

I'm (I am)	
You	
He	opening the door.
She	getting on the ladder.
It	coming down the ladder.
We	putting a foot on the moon.
They	
You	

Say it clearly!

coming
putting
opening
getting

You can describe the Present simple like this:

Subject	+ verb	(+ object)
Lions	eat	meat.
I	play	the piano.

How can you describe the Present continuous?

Subject	+	+	+ ....
He	is	coming down	the ladder.
We	are	waiting for	the eclipse.

Compare your ideas with other students' ideas.

3.3 Play a game: On the moon

Choose a verb and mime it to the class. They have to guess what you are doing.

open the rocket door   come down the ladder   walk on the moon   look at the Earth
drive the moon-car   put up the flag   eat space food   close the door   start the rocket

> You're starting the rocket!

> You're opening the door!

> You're eating space food!

> No, I'm not!

Be careful with spelling!
Verbs like 'put' and 'get' have a double 't' in the Present continuous: 'putting', 'getting'.

---

4   Comparing things

Short adjectives:
comparatives and
superlatives
Extra practice • WB Ex. 3
Extra practice • TB Ws. 10.2

4.1 Pluto is smaller than Earth

How do you say these sentences in your language?

Pluto is small.   The sun is big.
Pluto is smaller than Earth.   The sun is bigger than Earth.
Pluto is the smallest planet.   The sun is the biggest thing in the solar system.

In English, with short adjectives like 'small' and 'big', you use '-er' and 'the –est'
when you want to compare something.

But 'good' and 'bad' are different!

Walking is good for you.
Jogging is better than walking.
Running is the best.

The weather in England is bad.
The weather in Alaska is worse.
The weather in the Arctic Circle is the worst.

Arctic circle

4.2 PRACTICE

What can you say about these things?

HOT
… is hotter than …
… is the hottest.

Earth 30°C
Mercury 430°C
The Sun 6,000°C

LONG
A year on Earth is …
   a year on Mercury.
A year on Pluto is …

Mercury: 88 days
The Earth: 365 days
Pluto: 90,520 days

Kilimanjaro: 5,900 m
K2: 8,600 m
Mount Everest: 8,850 m

HIGH
K2 is … Kilimanjaro.
Mount Everest is …

BAD
A dog bite is … for you.
A snake bite is …
A shark bite is …!

GOOD
Science … for you.
History is …
English is …!

 Listen to the cassette to check your answers.

4.3   A quiz: Back on Earth

How much do you know about the world? You have three minutes.
Work with your neighbour and try to answer as many questions as possible.

1 The tallest building in the world is …
2 The biggest city in the world is …
3 The tallest animal in the world is …
4 The closest planet is …
5 The smallest country in the world is …
6 The fastest animal in the world is …

7 The pyramids in Egypt are older than Mount Everest. True or false?
8 The population of England is bigger than the population of your country. True or false?
9 London is smaller than New York. True or false?

Do you know any more 'tallest/smallest/fastest/biggest' facts? Ask the students in the class!

Be careful with spelling! Adjectives like 'hot' and 'big' double their last letter in the comparative: 'ho**tt**er' and 'bi**gg**er'.

5   Out and about with English

Travel: asking for information

Extra practice • LS Ex. 1

5.1 Mona, Sophie and Ali go to the circus

There is a circus near their town and Mona, Sophie and Ali want to go. They want to find out about the bus. They go to the bus station. They want to know:

the number of the bus   what time the bus comes back
what time the bus goes   the cost of the tickets

What questions do you think they ask?

5.2 Listen

Listen to Mona, Sophie and Ali at the bus station.
Do they ask your questions?

MAN:	Yes?
MONA:	Can you tell us which bus goes to Bletchley sportsground?
MAN:	Bletchley sportsground. Well, you can take number 34.
ALI:	The circus starts at half past three. What time is the bus?
MAN:	You can take one at half past one or half past two.
MONA:	What time does the bus come back? After six o'clock?
MAN:	You can take one at half past six or seven o'clock.
SOPHIE:	How much is the ticket?
MAN:	Single or return?
SOPHIE:	Return.
MAN:	£1.80.
MONA:	Thanks very much.
MAN:	You're welcome.
SOPHIE:	Bye.

Now you try it. Work with a partner.
One of you wants some information. The other one works in the bus station.
Choose one card each. Write in your own information.

CARD 1

West Town
BUS COMPANY

From West Town to East Town: Bus Number ....

Times from Newtown: ....

Times from Oldtown: ....

Price: single: .... return: ....

CARD 2

NORTH TOWN MOTORS

From North Town to South Town: Bus Number ....

Times from Hilltop: ....

Times from Weston: ....

Price: single: .... return: ....

Now ask your partner. Find out his/her information
and write it on the other card. (Don't look!)

Can you tell me which bus goes to …?
What time is the bus?
What time does the bus come back?
How much is the ticket?

When you are finished, check that you are right!

Act out your dialogue for the class.

---

6 Your Language Record

Now complete your *Language Record*.

Time to spare? Choose one of these exercises.

1 Write an exercise for your class *Exercise Box* (use the *Ideas list* on
  pages 88–89) or choose one to do. Check your answers on the back of
  the paper.

2 Look around your class. What are people doing *now*. Write six sentences.
  For example:
    Peter is reading his book.
    Maria is talking to David.

3 Think about your family and friends. Write six sentences about you and them.
  For example:
    Peter is older than me.
    Maria has longer hair than me.
    I am the tallest person in my family.

Language Record

Your own phrase book. ASKING FOR TRAVEL INFORMATION
Add more phrases. Write the meaning in your language.

Which bus goes to …?	Single ....
What time does the bus go?	Return ....
What time does the bus come back?	
How much is the ticket?	

The Present continuous. Complete the tables. Add some more examples.

I'm (I'm not)		Am I	
You are (aren't)		Are you	
He	reading a book.	...... he	
She	writing a letter.	...... she	coming?
It	making a drink.	...... it	speaking clearly?
They	singing a song.	...... they	sitting in your chair?
You		you	

Comparatives and superlatives. Complete the table.

Adjective	Comparative	Superlative
big	bigger	the biggest
high	......	......
......	taller	......
......	......	the longest
......	better	......
bad	......	......

Write some examples.

I am older than Peter.

....
....
....
....

Revision Box Prepositions

1 Prepositions tell us where something is. Fill in the missing word.

The monkey is … the box.   *next to*

2 Prepositions also tell you when something happens. Fill in the missing words.

I go to school …   MON   NOVEMBER

3 Play Preposition Bingo!
Complete the sentence. Choose one word for each gap.

I can meet you				
… the clock tower		… o'clock	on the first …	in …
under	behind	at 9 at 11	Wednesday Friday	June August
next to	in front of	at 10 at 12	Thursday Saturday	July September

If your teacher says your place, time, day or month, put a tick (√).
The first person to meet your teacher is the winner.

11 Topic The cavepeople

Cavepeople; curriculum
links with History and
Social Studies

1 15,000 years ago ...

Extra Practice • WB Ex. 1

15,000 years ago, people lived in caves.
Look at the picture.
How was life
for cavepeople?
Tell the class
your ideas.

exciting   boring
horrible   nice
dangerous   safe
hard   easy
difficult
happy
unhappy

I think it was exciting.

I think cavepeople were happy.

Say it clearly!

was /wɒz/
were /wə/

2 In a cave

Close your eyes and listen. What can you hear? Make a list.

I can hear ...

Compare your list with your neighbour and with the class. Do you
think the cave is a nice place? Is it dry or wet? Is it cold or warm?

Say it clearly!

I can hear /aɪ kən hɪə/

3 A dangerous life for cavepeople!

Reading

Life was very dangerous for cavepeople.
Why? Brainstorm your ideas
with your neighbour.

It was very
cold in winter

A
dangerous
life for
cavepeople

Now read the text. How many dangers
can you find? Can you add any more to your ideas above?

Nogoba – the cavegirl

Nogoba was a cavegirl. She lived in a cave with about 40 other people. Cavepeople lived in big groups to help each other. Their lives were very dangerous. There were many wild animals near the caves – lions, tigers, bears and elephants. The cavemen hunted. They killed the animals for food.

The children's jobs were dangerous, too. Nogoba and her friends went to the river every day to get water. Sometimes, the river was very deep. Sometimes, there were animals near the river.

For many months of the year, Nogoba was cold. There was ice and snow everywhere. It was difficult to be warm. The children sometimes went to sleep by the fire. Sometimes they were too near the fire.

Sometimes Nogoba and her friends went to find fruit and nuts to eat. Sometimes the fruit and nuts were poisonous and everyone became ill. There weren't any cave doctors or cave hospitals!

You can listen to the text on the cassette.

4 A dangerous life today

There are many dangers in modern life.
Brainstorm your ideas with the class.

Writing

5 Differences Poster

How is life different today?
Make a 'Differences Poster'.

Write your
sentences
on the poster.

Put your poster
on the wall.
During the next
lessons write some
more sentences on your poster.

Making a poster

Say it clearly!

lived
walked

6 Sing a song! Caveman Rock

🔲 Listen to 'Caveman Rock' and
sing it with your class. The words are on page 91.

7 Cavepeople painted and hunted

Reading

Extra reading • WB

Ex. 2–3

Extra practice • LS

Ex. 1–2

Work with a partner. One of you read 'Cave paintings' and the other
one read 'Hunting and cavepeople'.

How many questions can you each answer from your text?

Try to guess the words you don't know.

1 How did they make paint?
2 How did the cavepeople kill animals?
3 What did they put on their bodies? Why?
4 What animals did they hunt?
5 Where did they paint the pictures?

6 What part of the animal did they eat first?
7 Where did they keep their paint?
8 Why did they paint animals upside down?
9 When did they paint pictures?
10 What did they use for clothes?

Cave paintings

There are cave paintings in caves in many
different countries. Cavepeople painted
pictures of the animals that they hunted.
Cavepeople hunted mammoths, tigers and
bears. They painted the pictures inside their
cave. Sometimes the cavepeople painted the
animals upside down to show that the
animals were dead. They made their paint
from different plants to make green, yellow
and brown. They kept their paint in animal
bones. They painted their pictures before and
after a big hunt.

Hunting and cavepeople

Cavepeople hunted together in a big group. They
hunted mammoths, tigers and bears. They put animal
fat on their bodies. The fat helped to keep them warm
and it was difficult for the animals to hold them. They
also used the animal fat for lights. In the night, they
made terrible sounds and the animals were frightened.
The animals went into a river or sometimes they went
over a big cliff. The cavepeople killed the animals with
spears. They liked to eat the soft meat first (the heart
and the brains) and then they cooked the body of the
animal. They used the skins to make clothes.

Compare your answers with other students in your class.

🔲 You can listen to the texts on the cassette.

8 Decide ...

You can work by yourself, with a partner or in a small group. Choose an exercise.

Exercise 8.1 practises speaking and writing some Past tense verbs in a game.
Exercise 8.2 practises reading and writing.

Or you can do **something else**. Talk to your teacher and decide what to do.
(You can use the *Ideas list* on Pages 88–89 to make an exercise.)

8.1 Play a game: Danger!

Speaking and reading

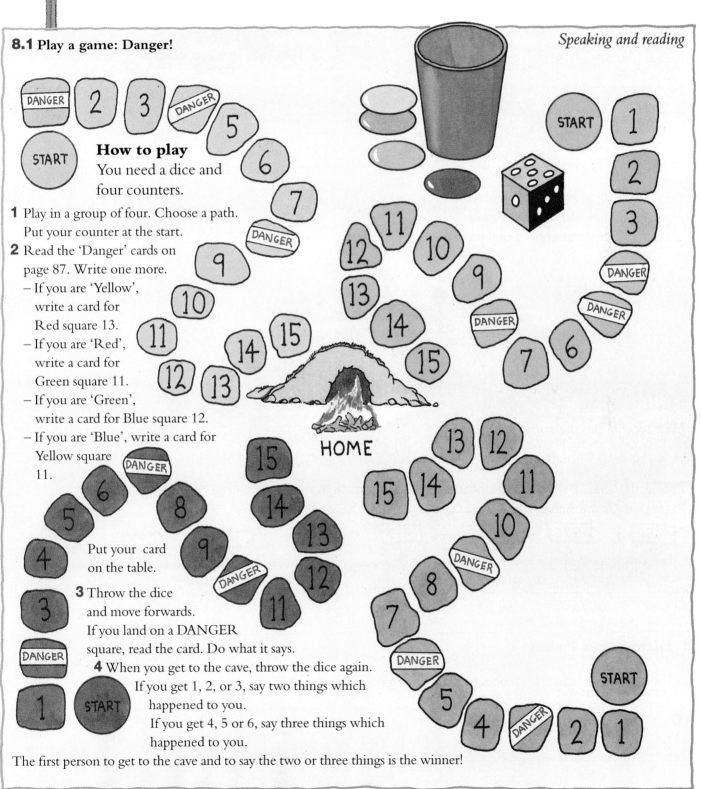

How to play
You need a dice and four counters.

1 Play in a group of four. Choose a path. Put your counter at the start.
2 Read the 'Danger' cards on page 87. Write one more.
   – If you are 'Yellow', write a card for Red square 13.
   – If you are 'Red', write a card for Green square 11.
   – If you are 'Green', write a card for Blue square 12.
   – If you are 'Blue', write a card for Yellow square 11.
   Put your card on the table.
3 Throw the dice and move forwards. If you land on a DANGER square, read the card. Do what it says.
4 When you get to the cave, throw the dice again. If you get 1, 2, or 3, say two things which happened to you. If you get 4, 5 or 6, say three things which happened to you.

The first person to get to the cave and to say the two or three things is the winner!

8.2 What changed first?

The life of cavepeople changed. Decide when the changes happened.
Match the sentences a–e with the numbers 1–5 on the timeline.

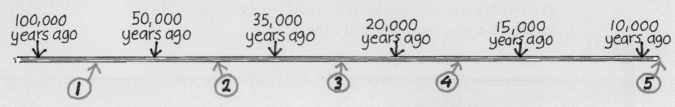

100,000 years ago   50,000 years ago   35,000 years ago   20,000 years ago   15,000 years ago   10,000 years ago

① ② ③ ④ ⑤

a They painted pictures on the walls of the caves.
They had pots for water and food.

b They picked fruit and killed animals for food.
They moved to a different place every night.

c They lived in small houses.
They had sheep and goats.
They had wool for clothes.

d They lived in caves. They had stone
tools and skin bags for their tools.

e They lived in villages.
They were farmers and had
fruit and vegetables for food.

Your teacher has the correct answers.

Can you draw a timeline for 150 years ago until now? Guess when these things happened.

People had cars.   People used telephones.   People used electricity.   People used computers.
People went to the moon.   People went by train.   People went to school.

1850   1870   1890   1910   1930   1950   1970   1990

Add more things to your timeline.

9 Differences Poster

Can you add some more sentences to your Differences Poster now?

10   Your Language Record

Now complete your *Language Record*.

Language Record

Write or draw the meaning of the words. Add the missing examples.

Word	Meaning	Example
a cave		
a picture		
fat		
skin		The cavepeople used animal skin to make clothes.
dangerous		
dark		It is very dark inside the caves.
deep		It is dangerous to swim in deep water.
exciting		It was exciting to hunt an animal.
frightened		The animals were frightened of the sounds.
happy		
upside down		Cavepeople painted animals upside down.
wild		
chase		The hunters chased the animals into the river.
hunt		
kill		They killed animals with spears.
paint		
pick		The children picked nuts and fruit to eat.
show		They painted the animals upside down to show they were dead.
went		The animals went into the river.

Choose some more words. Add their meanings and examples.

> poisonous   safe   ice   soft   attack   a cliff   a goat   a spear   a sheep

Time to spare? Choose one of these exercises.

1 Choose an exercise from your class *Exercise Box* or use the *Ideas list* on pages 88–89 to make an exercise for your class *Exercise Box*.

2 Are these sentences true (T) or false (F)?

  a Cave people were vegetarians. ☐   **c** They liked paintings. ☐

  b They cooked their food. ☐   **d** They had telephones. ☐

Write some more true/false sentences for other students.

3 Imagine … you are a caveperson. Draw a picture of yourself and where you live. Write about your life.

12 Language focus

1 Your own past: your first day at school

Discussion

Tell the class what you can remember.

What was the name of your first school?	*My first school was …*
Was it big or small?	*It was a small/big school.*
Can you remember your first classroom?	*The classrooms were …*
How many children were there?	*There were …*
Who was your teacher?	*My teacher's name was …*
How old were you?	*I was … years old.*

2 Sophie's first day

Listening

Barbara is asking Sophie about her first school.
Listen and answer the questions.

Where was Sophie's first school?
Was it big or small?
What was her classroom like?
How old was she?

BARBARA: Sophie, where did you go to school before?
SOPHIE: I went to a school in Scotland.
BARBARA: Was it nice?
SOPHIE: Yes, it was a very small school. It had 86 pupils.
BARBARA: That's very small!
SOPHIE: Yes, but there were a lot of children in each classroom. There were 32 in my classroom. There were only three classrooms.
BARBARA: Was it an old school?
SOPHIE: Yes, it was very old. It was more than 200 years old. We were in the best classroom. In the other rooms, in the winter, there was ice inside the rooms!
BARBARA: Oh! When did you start school?
SOPHIE: At nine o'clock.
BARBARA: No, I mean, how old were you?
SOPHIE: About four and half.
BARBARA: Oh. I was five, I think …

Was your first school bigger or smaller than Sophie's?
Was it older or newer? Were you younger or older than Sophie?

3 Were you older? Was it newer?

'was' and 'were'

Extra practice • WB

Ex. 2

Extra practice • TB

Ws. 12.1

3.1 'Was' and 'were'

When do you say 'was'? When do you say 'were'?
Look at these sentences from Units 11 and 12 and complete the table.

It was a small/big school
The classrooms were ....
I was four years old.
It was exciting.
It was dangerous.
Cavepeople were vegetarians.
Cavepeople were farmers.
Nogoba was a cavegirl.
The river was very deep.

It was very cold.
Life was very exciting.
Cavepeople were happy.
Cavemen were hunters.
It was difficult.
Sometimes, everyone was ill.
How old were you?
Were you happy there?
We were in the best classroom.

I	....	
You	....	older.
He + She+ It + }	....	happy. 12 years old. very cold.
We	....	
They	....	
There	....	32 children in my classroom.
There	....	ice in the classroom.

3.2 Was it cold?

Choose the best question to continue each conversation.

a I went swimming on Saturday.
b I went to the cinema at the weekend.
c I went to bed at 6 o'clock last night.
d I went in a helicopter yesterday.
e We walked home last night.
f My mother helped me with my homework yesterday.
g I cooked a meal yesterday.

1 Was it a long way?
2 Were you excited?
3 Was the film good?
4 Were you tired?
5 Was it difficult?
6 Was the water cold?
7 Was it good?

3.3 Spot the differences

Look at these pictures. Can you find eight
differences between the morning and the
afternoon? Write a sentence about each one.

In the afternoon

In the morning

4 Some more Past tense verbs

*Regular Past verbs;
'went', 'had', 'saw',
'made'*

Extra practice • WB Ex. 1, 3
Extra practice • LS Ex. 1
Extra practice • TB Ws. 12.1

4.1 What do you say?

Think about the Past tense in your language. Do many verbs in the Past look the same? Are there some verbs which are very different? Which verbs are they?

4.2 What's the difference?

Look at these sentences. Put a circle around each verb in List A and List B. How are the verbs different?

LIST A	LIST B
We walked home last night.	I walk home every night.
My mother helped me with my homework yesterday.	She always helps me with my homework.
I watched a horror film last night.	Usually, I never watch horror films.
I had a lot of homework last night.	I always have a lot on Monday night.
I saw Peter yesterday.	I usually see him on Thursday.
I went to bed at 6 o'clock last night.	I usually go to bed at 9 o'clock.
I made a cake yesterday.	I usually make a cake on Sunday.

4.3 Past verbs

In English, you add '-ed' to the end of many verbs to make the Past tense.

Complete the text with the Past tense of the verbs.

Cavepeople .... (live) more than 30,000 years ago. They .... (walk) from place to place and they .... (use) stones to make tools. They .... (hunt) in big groups and .... (kill) animals for their food. They .... (cook) the meat on a fire in front of their cave. Often, they .... (paint) pictures of the animals in their caves.

THE LIFE OF THE CAVEPEOPLE

Cave paintings from Lascaux

Say it clearly!

lived played used killed /d/
walked cooked /t/
painted hunted /ɪd/

CAVE MUSIC

Other verbs are very different. Look back at List A in 4.2 and complete these sentences.

Sometimes, the cavepeople .... (make) music with bones from animals. They .... (have) many pipes to blow and many things to bang. They .... (play) with their fingers. They .... (use) the pipes to tell each other about dangerous animals. They also .... (use) the pipes when they .... (go) hunting. If they .... (see) an animal, they .... (make) a lot of noise.

🎞 Listen to the texts on the cassette and check your answers.

Ask your neighbour.

What did you do
on Tuesday?

What did you do on
Monday last week?

What did you do
on Wednesday?

I went to ....

I played ....

I saw ....

I walked to ....

I made ....

5   Out and about with English

*Talking about
past events*

Extra practice • LS Ex. 2

5.1 **It was fun!**

Where do you like to go? Tell the class about somewhere
you went where you had fun.

*Last weekend …   Last month …   Last summer …
I went to …   I saw …   I made …   I had …   I played …   I was …*

They can ask you questions.

*Was it nice?   Where was it?   Was it exciting?   Was it big?
Were you frightened?   Were you with your friends?*

5.2 **Sophie's party**

Sophie and Mona are at a party.
Look at the picture. What do
you think they are saying?

5.3 **Listen. Are you right?**

Listen to Sophie and Mona.

S: Do you like the party?
M: Er … yes. I think so. I went to a
      different type of party last week.
S: Was there any music?
M: Yes. But it was different. There was a sitar.
S: What's that?
M: Like a big guitar … and a tabla …
S: What's that?
M: A special type of drum.
S: Was it a dancing party?
M: No, not really. Do you like dancing parties?
S: Yes! I went to a party last week, too.
M: Was it like this?

S: No. It was great. It was a swimming party.
M: A swimming party?!
S: Yes. We had races and games in the
      swimming pool.
M: Was it a birthday party?
S: Yes.
M: Was there a birthday cake?
S: Yes, but it went in the water!

Now you try it. Work with a partner. You can change Sophie and Mona's dialogue. Talk about something you did. Here are some ideas:

Last weekend …

Last month …

Last summer …

I went to …   I saw …

I made …   I had …

I played …   I was …

Was it noisy?   Was it quiet?   Was there dancing?

Was there music?   Were your friends there?

Was it a birthday party?   Was the food nice?

Act out your dialogue for the class.

6 Your Language Record

Now complete your *Language Record*.

Time to spare? Choose one of these exercises.

1 Choose an exercise from the *Exercise Box* or use the *Ideas list* on pages 88–89 to make an exercise for your class *Exercise Box*.

2 Write the Past tense of the verbs in the sentences.

a I .... in Japan for five years. (live)

b She .... the car on Sunday. (clean)

c He .... his hair last night. (wash)

d We .... at the party for three hours. (stay)

e The children .... television last night. (watch)

Write an exercise like this for other students.

3 What is the first thing you can remember? Write a few sentences.

The thing I can remember is when I was … years old.
I went/saw/made/visited/played …

Language Record

Your own phrase book! TALKING ABOUT PAST EVENTS

Add more phrases. Write the meaning in your language.

What did you do last night?	I made ....
I went to	I had ....
I saw	I played ....
....	What was it like? ....
	It was great. ....

Complete the table with 'was' and 'were'. Add some more examples.

I	was		There were ....
You	...		There was ....
He +		here yesterday.	....
She +	...	very cold last night.	....
It +		happy at school.	....
We	...		....
They	...		....

Complete the sentences.

'-ed' verbs.

Cavepeople .... from place to place. (walk)

They .... animals. (hunt)

They .... meat on a fire. (cook)

They .... in caves. (live)

They .... music together. (play)

Other verbs. Complete the sentences.

Cavepeople .... a very dangerous life. (have)

There .... many wild animals. (be)

If they .... an animal (see), they .... a terrible sound (make).

They .... after the animals and killed them.(go)

Revision Box Comparatives and superlatives

1 Can you complete the sentence? Write seven different sentences using the adjectives a–g.

Life is .... now but 15,000 years ago it was ....

a hard b quiet c easy d short e good f bad

2 Can you complete the sentence? Write five different sentences using the adjectives a–e.

A giraffe is .... but an elephant is probably the .... animal in the world.

a strong b big c fat d heavy

3 Work with a partner. Do you know any 'tallest/biggest/ strongest/fastest' facts? Write as many as you can. Use these words.

tall   The tallest mountain in the world is Mount Everest.

fast   short   good (the best)   bad (the worst)   small   high

deep   long   heavy   strong

Compare your facts with other students in your class. Who has the most?

A Optional Unit Activity
Making an Exercise Box

Writing exercises helps you learn English. In this Unit you can make a box
of exercises for other students to do.

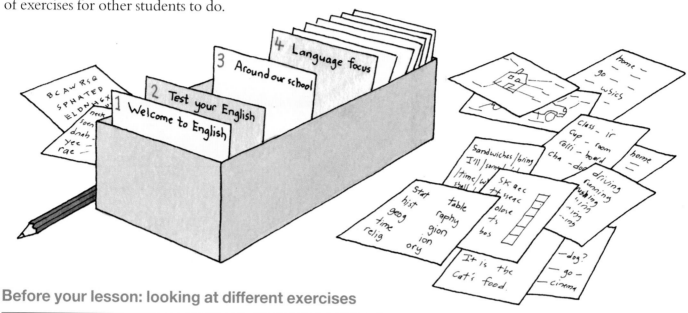

Before your lesson: looking at different exercises

1 Look back

Look through Units 1, 2, 3 and 4. Write down on which page there is:

- a vocabulary exercise
- a reading exercise
- a listening exercise
- a writing exercise

In your lesson: writing your exercises for the Exercise Box

2 Types of exercise

Show your neighbour which exercises you found. How many different
kinds of exercises can you find?

3 The Ideas list

Here are three types of exercises.
Can you find the same types of exercises
in the *Ideas list* on pages 88–89?

Word halves

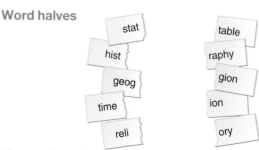

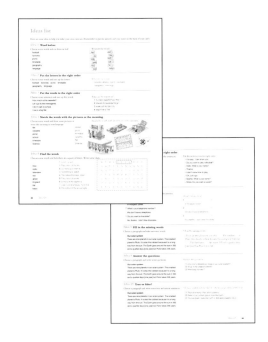

A word puzzle

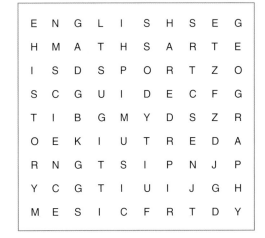

E	N	G	L	I	S	H	S	E	G
H	M	A	T	H	S	A	R	T	E
I	S	D	S	P	O	R	T	Z	O
S	C	G	U	I	D	E	C	F	G
T	I	B	G	M	Y	D	S	Z	R
O	E	K	I	U	T	R	E	D	A
R	N	G	T	S	I	P	N	J	P
Y	C	G	T	I	U	I	J	G	H
M	E	S	I	C	F	R	T	D	Y

Mixed-up sentences

1 I very can play well football

2 a factory near school our There is

3 are ? How you

Work in a small group. Make up some exercises for other students to do.

Word halves: find 12 new words and divide them. Mix them up. Write the meaning in your language or draw a small picture.

Word puzzle: choose eight words and put them in a letter square.

Mixed-up sentences: find eight sentences. Mix up the words.

Write a title for the exercises (for example: Word halves) and put your name on it. Write the answers on the back of the paper. Put the exercises in the box.

4   Take an exercise

Take an exercise from the box. See if you can do it. Don't write on the paper! You can check your answers on the back.

5   Evaluation

Discuss these questions with the people in the class.

Is it difficult to write exercises?

Were the exercises in the box easy to understand?

How can you write better exercises next time?

B Optional Unit Activity A Parcel of English

Before your lesson

1 Pictures of you and your town

Draw a small picture of yourself
(5 cm × 5 cm) or find a passport photo.
Find some postcards and photographs
of your town to take to your lesson.

You also need glue, scissors and small
pieces of paper.

In your lesson

2 A Parcel of English

Look at the picture of a Parcel of English on page 7. Discuss these questions with your class.

What is in the parcel?   What can you do with your parcel?

Can you display it in your school?

Can you give it to a class in your school or send it to another school in another country?

3 What's in the Parcel of English?

What can you put in your Parcel of English? With your class, make a list of your ideas.
(If you want to post your Parcel of English, remember that it can't be very big!)

You and your class
photographs

Your school
timetables

Your town
postcards

4 A picture and description of me

For the first part of your Parcel of English, you can
write a short description of yourself. For example:

My name is ... . I am ... old.
I have ... . I like ... and I can ... .

Look at Unit 1 Exercise 4 for help.

Put your picture on the small piece of paper from
your teacher. Write your description next to it.

Your teacher will put all your descriptions together.

5 Writing in groups

Divide into groups of three or four students. First, with your class decide which part of the Parcel of English (a–d) each group will write.

YOUR TOWN
a Where people work
b Where people go in their free time

YOUR SCHOOL
c A description of your school
d The subjects and timetable

🔊 Listen to these examples.

About our town

Where people work in our town

In our town, people work in car factories. They make cars. Some people work in shops in the city centre and some people work in hotels. A lot of people work at the airport.

Where people go in their free time

In our town, people go to the cinema in their free time at weekends. Some people go dancing. Many people do sports – football, swimming, and bicycle riding. A lot of people go to restaurants and cafés.

About our school

A description of our school

Our school is in the north of the city near the airport and factories. It is very big. There are 40 rooms and 700 students in the school. We've got a football field, three laboratories and a computer room. Our classroom is near the computer room.

Our school day

We go to school six days a week. We start lessons at 8 o'clock and we go home at 3 o'clock. We have lunch from 12 o'clock to 1 o'clock. We have 8 lessons every day. One lesson is 40 minutes. The students come to school when they are 11 years old.

Work in your group. Read the examples again. Talk about and write your part of the parcel. Help each other with words and spellings. (Everybody in your group must write.)

6 Put it together

Now put your work on a piece of paper with your pictures. If you have time, you can write about the pictures.

7 Your Parcel of English!

Look at Exercise 3 again. For your next lesson, bring more things for your Parcel of English. Put them with your pictures and writing.

You now have a Parcel of English to send to another school!

Optional Unit Revision

1 What do they do?

'doesn't' and 'don't'

Write about the students.

	Question	Yes	No
🎹	**1** Do you play the piano?	✓	✓✓✓✓✓✓
🏐	**2** Do you play football?	✓✓✓✓✓✓	✓
🏢	**3** Do you live in a flat?	✓✓✓✓✓	✓✓
⚗️	**4** Do you like Science?	✓✓✓✓✓✓	✓
🐎	**5** Do you ride a horse?	✓	✓✓✓✓✓✓
🚶	**6** Do you walk to school?	✓✓✓✓✓✓	✓

1 One student plays the piano. Seven students don't play the piano.

2 Seven students .... One student doesn't ....

3 ....

4 ....

5 ....

6 ....

2 What's the question?

Present simple questions

A Here are some questions about elephants. Join them to the right answer.

1 How long does an elephant live?

2 What do they eat?

3 What do they look like?

4 Where do they live?

5 How many hours do they sleep?

a They have big ears, thick skin, and a long trunk.

b In Africa and India.

c For about sixty years.

d Fruit, leaves and grass.

e About four hours.

B Praying mantids are very strange animals. What questions can you ask about them?

1 Where ....   4 ....

2 What ....   5 ....

3 How ....   6 ....

C Now read about praying mantids. How many of your questions can you answer?

PRAYING MANTIDS are a type of insect. They live in many parts of the world, including the rainforests of South America and the deserts of Africa. They eat small insects and spiders but some big mantids eat small frogs and birds. Some mantids eat other mantids. They start with the head first so that they cannot get away. Mantids come in many different colours. Some of them are very beautiful. The flower mantids from Africa look like flowers. Insects land on them to get food but, instead, the mantids eat them! Mantids live for about five to seven years.

3 This is my family

Fill in the missing word. Look back at your *Language Record* for help.

1
Hello.
_ _ name's Tom.

2
This is _ _ sister.
_ _ _ name's Sally.

3
And this is _ _ brother.
_ _ _ name's Jack.

4
Here are _ _ parents.
_ _ _ _ _ names are Peter and Susan.

5
This is _ _ fish.
_ _ _ name is Jaws.

6
This is _ _ _ house.

7
What's _ _ _ _ name?

4 What's the word?

	1	3		7			15
			4 5	8		13	
				9			

2 T H E **6** N A T U R A L **10** **11 12** W O R L D **14**

1 Lions eat ....

2 People sleep for about eight ....

3 An .... has six legs.

4 An animal that lives in Australia.

5 Giraffes eat ....

6 Birds live in ....

7 A humming bird is a b... animal.

8 A parrot is a type of ....

9 Dolphins and whales are ....

10 Wild animals that live in Africa.

11 Fish live in ....

12 We are mammals. .... blood is warm.

13 Bats sleep .... the day.

14 How .... do cows live?

15 They eat bamboo.

D Optional Unit Revision

1 Food puzzle

Vocabulary

Find these things in the puzzle.

1 three foods with carbohydrates
2 three foods with fats
3 three foods with protein
4 three foods with fibre
5 two foods with minerals

```
O I L E D G E E L R E T V
M E A T Y J K I O O X E E
B R E A D B I N G T A G G
N U T S M I L K V A C M E
E G G S R R I C E T T I T
B E A N S B O Z R E E S A
R A B C H E E S E M L R B
A T L P O T A T O E S T L
S D R G V F I S H C O D E
C E R E A L S T E B R R S
E E H Q B U T T E R A E W
```

2 Some more practice

Work with your neighbour and do these exercises.

A Say what you think

Write your answer.

1 What do you think of football?
I .... it.
I think it's ....

2 Do you like cats?
....
....

3 What do you think of Maths?
....
....

4 Do you like snakes?
....
....

5 Do you like this boat?
....
....

6 What do you think of this woman?
....
....

B 'some' and 'any'

What's on the table?
Write some sentences, like this:

bread – cheese

There is some bread and some cheese.

sugar – eggs

There is some sugar but there aren't any eggs.

1 milk – salt

2 cheese – fish

3 butter – sugar

4 water – flour

....

....

C 'me/you/him/her/us/them'

Fill in the gaps.

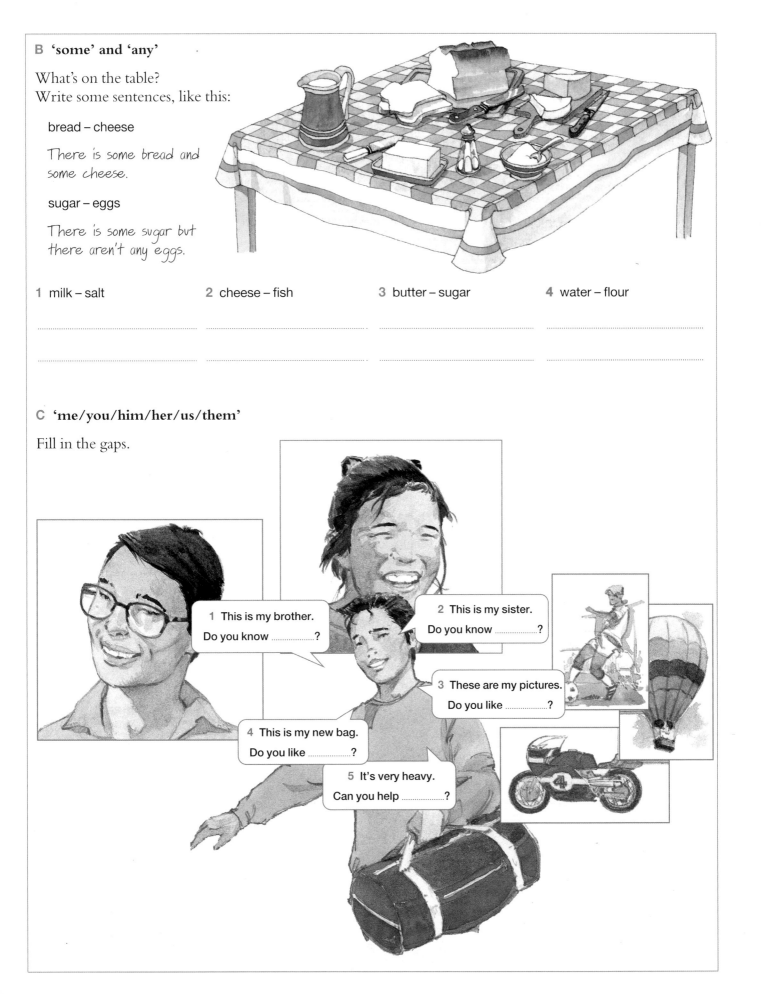

1 This is my brother.
Do you know .... ?

2 This is my sister.
Do you know .... ?

3 These are my pictures.
Do you like .... ?

4 This is my new bag.
Do you like .... ?

5 It's very heavy.
Can you help .... ?

Optional Unit Activity
Poems from the Earth and space

1 The words in your head

Think about the stars, planets and space, and write down the words and phrases you can remember. You can listen to the cassette while you think. It has some more of Holst's *The Planets Suite*.

Pluto — SPACE — The sun is very hot

The sky is history — stars — The moon

2 Talk to your neighbour

Show your words to your neighbour and look back at Unit 9. Do you want to add any words? Talk to your neighbour about what your words mean.

3 Imagine ...

You are travelling in space. You can see the Earth from your rocket. What more can you see? What can you hear? Is it nice in space or horrible? Is it exciting?

Imagine that the Earth can speak. What does it say? Is it happy? Is it sad? What does it like? What does it want? What does it think? Tell the rest of the class your ideas.

4 Write a poem

Write a poem about your ideas. You can imagine that you are travelling from the Earth or you can imagine that the Earth speaks. Read your poem and make changes as you write.

Listen to some examples.

I am old.
I am very old.
Millions of people live on me.
I give them food.
I give them air.
I give them life.

I can see the stars in the sky.
Millions of stars.
The moon looks at me.
The sun shines.
I can see space.
Space, space, space.
Lots of space!

For more ideas, show your poem to your neighbour and look back at Unit 9.
You can write your poem in a shape.

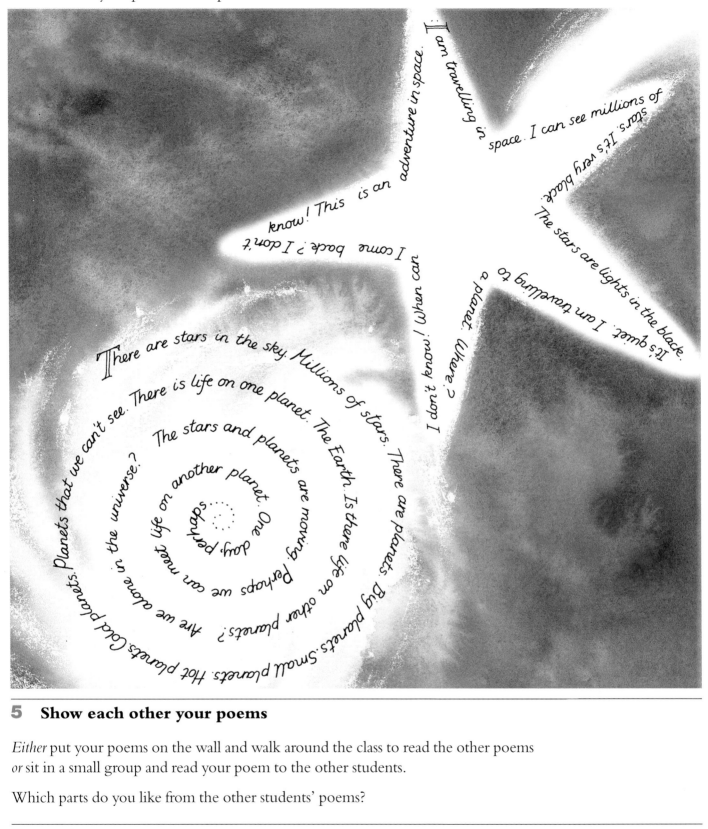

There are stars in the sky. Millions of stars. There are planets. Big planets. Small planets. Hot planets. Cold planets. Planets that we can't see. There is life on one planet. The Earth. Is there life on other planets? Are we alone in the universe? The stars and planets are moving. Perhaps we can meet life on another planet. One day, perhaps.

I am travelling in space. I can see millions of stars. It's very black. The stars are lights in the black. It's quiet. I am travelling to a planet. Where? I don't know! When can I come back? I don't know! This is an adventure in space. I am ...

5 Show each other your poems

Either put your poems on the wall and walk around the class to read the other poems
or sit in a small group and read your poem to the other students.

Which parts do you like from the other students' poems?

6 Evaluation

Was it easy or difficult to write the poems? Did you like writing poems?
Would you like to do it again? How? Alone? In a group? In your book? On a poster?

F Optional Unit Revision

1 Some more practice

A test

How much do you know? Work with your neighbour.

A Was/Were

Fill in the gaps in this text with 'was' or 'were'.

We know that cavepeople ___1___ good artists. But they ___2___
also good musicians. Their pipes ___3___ animal bones.

The leg bone ___4___ the best pipe. When the bone ___5___ dry, the cavepeople
made some holes in it. When the pipe ___6___ ready, they played some music.

B Write about the past

Use these verbs to write about what Anna did at the weekend.

*On Saturday, Anna watched television.
Then she …*

Saturday	Sunday
television (watch)	car (clean)
mother (help)	friend (talk)
a cake (make)	a film (see)

C What's the word?

Find the word in the square. They go across (→) and down (↓).

1

2 Cavepeople painted p.................

3 r.................

4 Cavepeople h.................
   for their food.

5 They killed the animals
   with s.................

6 u.................
   d.................

A	B	D	C	A	V	E	H	J	J	K	U	N
G	T	E	F	E	T	R	E	Y	O	A	J	H
U	P	S	I	D	E	A	D	O	W	N	E	U
R	A	J	K	E	U	H	J	E	V	M	A	N
I	W	S	P	E	A	R	S	Q	P	M	A	T
V	S	H	W	J	U	A	N	Q	D	K	M	E
E	A	P	I	C	T	U	R	E	S	Y	W	D
R	K	J	O	K	E	O	M	H	A	G	F	E

D Write five sentences about the life of someone you know well – a friend,
a famous person or someone in your family or yourself!

Now check your answers on page 87.

Danger cards

These are the cards for the Exercise 8.1 game on page 67.

4

An elephant attacked you. Go to 1.

5

You were ill. Go to 2.

2

It rained very hard. Miss a turn.

7

A tiger chased you. Go to 4.

8

You talked to a friend. Miss a turn.

11

....
....
....

10

You killed a bear. Go to 12.

13

....
....
....

3

You picked a lot of fruit on trees. Go to 8.

6

A dangerous person from another group chased you. Go back to 2.

1

You went to a party at another cave. Miss a turn.

4

You had some bad fruit. Go to 2.

9

You went into the river. Miss a turn.

12

....
....
....

8

You went fishing all day. Go to 5.

11

....
....
....

Answers to Optional Unit F, Exercise 2

C The words are: cave, pictures, river, hunted, spears, upside down.

B On Saturday, Anna watched television. Then she helped her mother and made a cake. On Sunday, she cleaned the car and talked to a friend. She also saw a film.

A 1 were 2 were 3 were 4 was 5 was 6 was

Ideas list

Here are some ideas to help you make your own exercises. (Remember to put the answers and your name on the back of your card.)

Idea 1 Word halves

Choose some words and cut them in half.

football
factories
picnic
timetable
geography
language

What are the words?

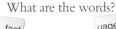

fact
pic
lang
geog
foot
time

uage
ories
table
ball
nic
raphy

Idea 2 Put the letters in the right order

Choose some words and mix up the letters.

football factories picnic timetable
geography language

What are the words?

casioftre albofotl icpcin meibalett
haoggrepy aaeulngg

Idea 3 Put the words in the right order

Choose some sentences and mix up the words.

How much is this cassette?
Let's go to the newsagents.
I don't walk to school.
I live in a big flat.

What are the sentences?

1 is much cassette how this ?
2 the lets to newsagents go
3 walk I school don't to
4 big in live a I flat

Idea 4 Match the words with the pictures or the meaning

Choose some words and draw some pictures or write the meaning in your language.

flat	school
cassette	picnic
picnic	timetable
school	cassette
timetable	flat
Science	Science

Match the words with the pictures or the meaning.

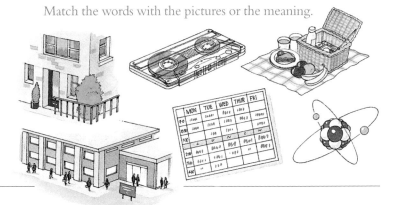

Idea 5 Find the words

Choose some words and hide them in a square of letters. Write some clues.

blue
radio
television
red
green
England
flat
black

Find the words.

1 The colour of the sky.
2 Something to listen to.
3 Something to watch.
4 The colour that says 'Stop!'.
5 The colour of leaves.
6 London is the capital of ....
7 I don't live in a house. I live in a ....
8 The colour of the sky at night.

R	E	D	T	B	L	U	E	Y	U	F
S	G	R	E	E	N	B	N	M	K	L
R	A	D	I	O	E	L	L	O	W	A
C	V	B	N	M	B	R	T	E	N	T
E	N	G	L	A	N	D	U	I	O	P
D	C	B	L	A	C	K	G	G	B	F
T	E	L	E	V	I	S	I	O	N	U

Idea 6 Put the sentences in the right order

Choose a dialogue or a paragraph. Mix up the sentences.

MONA: Hello. What's your name?
SOPHIE: Sophie. What's your name?
MONA: Mona. Do you want a sweet?
SOPHIE: Thanks.
MONA: Do you want to play volleyball?
SOPHIE: I don't know how to play.
MONA: It's easy. I can show you.
SOPHIE: OK. Let's go.

Put the sentences in the right order.

– It's easy. I can show you.
– Do you want to play volleyball?
– Hello. What's your name?
– Thanks.
– I don't know how to play.
– OK. Let's go.
– Sophie. What's your name?
– Mona. Do you want a sweet?

Idea 7 What's the question?

Write some questions and answers. Copy the answers.
Leave space for the questions.

1 Where do you live?

   In Prospect Street.

2 What's your telephone number?

   We don't have a telephone.

3 Do you want a chocolate?

   No, thanks. I don't like chocolate.

What's the question?

1 ....?

   In Prospect Street.

2 ....?

   We don't have a telephone.

3 ....?

   No, thanks. I don't like chocolate.

Idea 8 Fill in the missing words

Choose a paragraph and take out some words.

Our solar system
There are nine planets in our solar system. The smallest
planet is Pluto. It is also the coldest because it is a long
way from the sun. The Earth goes around the sun in 365
and a quarter days [one year] but Pluto takes 248 years.

Fill in the missing words.

There are nine planets in our solar .... The smallest ...... is Pluto.
It is also the coldest because it is a long way from the .... The
Earth goes ...... the sun in 365 and a quarter days [one year] but
Pluto takes 248 ....

Idea 9 Answer the questions

Choose a paragraph and write some questions.

Our solar system
There are nine planets in our solar system. The smallest
planet is Pluto. It is also the coldest because it is a long
way from the sun. The Earth goes around the sun in 365
and a quarter days [one year] but Pluto takes 248 years.

Answer the questions.

1 How many planets are there in our solar system?
2 What is the smallest planet?
3 How long is a year?

Idea 10 True or false?

Choose a paragraph and write some true and untrue sentences.

Our solar system
There are nine planets in our solar system. The smallest
planet is Pluto. It is also the coldest because it is a long
way from the sun. The Earth goes around the sun in 365
and a quarter days [one year] but Pluto takes 248 years.

Are these sentences true, false or is the information not in the text?

1 There are many other solar systems.
2 Pluto is the furthest planet from the Earth.
3 The sun goes round the Earth in 365 and a quarter days.

Songs

Unit 1 'I'm so happy'

I've got lots of friends
in my school.
I've got lots of friends
in my town.
I've got lots of
things to do.
I've got lots of
things to say.

I'm so happy,
Life's so good.
I'm so happy,
Life's so good.

There is music in my house.
There is music in my school.
There is sunshine in my street.
There is sunshine in my town.

I'm so happy,
Life's so good.
I'm so happy,
Life's so good.

I've got lots of friends in my school.
I've got lots of friends in my town.
I've got lots of things to do.
I've got lots of things to say.

I'm so happy,
Life's so good.

Unit 3 'In my town, in the countryside'

In my town there are shops
And there's a railway station.
I go there and I buy
A ticket for my destination.
I'm going to the countryside,
I'm going to the countryside.
I love it, I love it, I love it.
Birds and hills and big blue skies,
In the countryside

In the countryside there are farms,
There are animals too.
But all my friends live in my town
So this is what I do:
I go back to my town,
I go back to my town.
I love it, I love it, I love it.
Cars and people all around,
In my town.
I love it, I love it, I love it.
Birds and hills and
big blue skies,
In the countryside. *etc.*

Unit 5 'Wimoweh'

Wimoweh, wimoweh,
Wimoweh, wimoweh, *etc.*

In the jungle, the mighty jungle,
The lion sleeps tonight.

In the jungle the mighty fire,
The fire burns bright tonight.

Hush my darling,
Don't cry my darling,
The lion sleeps tonight.

Wimoweh, wimoweh,
Wimoweh, wimoweh, *etc.*

Unit 7 'I love chocolate'

I drink milk, I eat cheese,
I like nuts and I like greens,
I like cereals, I like beans,
These are things my body needs.

Chorus
But late at night,
Under my bedclothes,
I eat chocolate,
And no-one knows.

I eat vegetables, I drink juice,
I like rice, I like fruit,
I like pasta every way,
I eat good things every day.

Repeat chorus

I like honey on my bread,
I like salad and I like eggs,
I drink water all day long,
All these things make me strong.

Repeat chorus

Unit 9 'Space'

In the night, night sky
I can see
Bright, bright lights
Are shining on you and me,
And in the bright, bright lights
There are creatures too,
In their night, night skies,
They're looking at me and you.

Chorus
The moon, the stars, the universe,
It's a beautiful place,
The planets and the galaxies,
Space, space, space.

So tonight, night, night,
Now you know,
Look at the bright, bright lights,
Look up and say 'Hello'.

Repeat chorus

Every night, I say 'Hi'
To my neighbours in the sky,
Every night I sing my song,
Everybody sing along:

I live on Planet Zaarb,
Can anybody hear?
I live on planet Zaarb,
Does anyone know I'm here?

Final chorus
The moon, the stars, the universe,
It's a beautiful place,
The planets and the galaxies,
I live out here in space, space!

Unit 11 'Caveman rock'

I'm a caveman and I'm OK,
I'm a caveman and I hunt all day,
I haven't got a car and I haven't got a flat,
I haven't got a dog or a pussy cat,
I'm a caveman and I'm OK.

I'm a caveman and I'm OK,
I'm a caveman and I hunt all day,
I keep my paint inside a bone,
I cut my meat with spears and stone,
I'm a caveman and I'm OK.

I'm a caveman and I'm OK,
I'm a caveman and I hunt all day,
I haven't got a fridge and I haven't got a bed,
I haven't got a Walkman on my head,
I'm a caveman and I'm OK.

I'm a caveman and I'm OK,
I'm a caveman and I hunt all day,
I keep quite warm with fire and skin,
I make the pots that we cook in,
I'm a caveman and I'm OK.

Map of the world

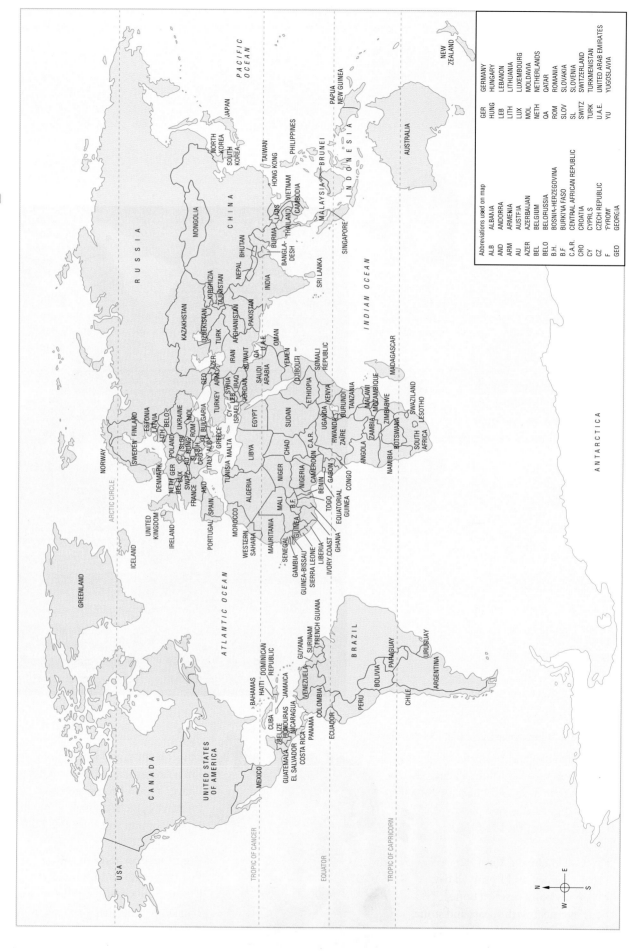

Abbreviations used on map

ALB	ALBANIA	GER	GERMANY
AND	ANDORRA	HUNG	HUNGARY
ARM	ARMENIA	LEB	LEBANON
AU	AUSTRIA	LITH	LITHUANIA
AZER	AZERBAIJAN	LUX	LUXEMBOURG
BEL	BELGIUM	MOL	MOLDAVIA
BELO	BELORUSSIA	NETH	NETHERLANDS
B.H.	BOSNIA-HERZEGOVINA	QA	QATAR
B.F	BURKINA FASO	ROM	ROMANIA
C.A.R.	CENTRAL AFRICAN REPUBLIC	SLOV	SLOVAKIA
CRO	CROATIA	SL	SLOVENIA
CY	CYPRLS	SWITZ	SWITZERLAND
CZ	CZECH REPUBLIC	TURK	TURKMENISTAN
F	'FYROM'	U.A.E.	UNITED ARAB EMIRATES
GEO	GEORGIA	YU	YUGOSLAVIA

Wordlist/Index

In this list you can find the words which appear in the *Topic*, *Language focus* and Optional Units and their page numbers. This list is also an index of the language and the grammar in the book.

Thanks and acknowledgements

Authors' thanks

The development of this course has been a large part of our lives for well over six years. During this time, we have become indebted to literally thousands of people who have so generously shared their time, skills and experience. In particular, we appreciate the constructive advice of the numerous teachers and students who helped with our initial classroom research and with the piloting, the readers, and the language teaching specialists. The final version owes much to their enthusiastic involvement.

We would like to record a special 'thank you' to Peter Donovan who shared our ideals of innovation and who has provided input and support throughout. Also to James Dingle, our editor, whose hard work, professionalism, understanding and painstaking attention to detail have helped transform our ideals into reality, and Sarah Brierly who so efficiently managed the production of the pilot editions of *Cambridge English for Schools*. The pride we now take in the design of the materials is due to the skilful contribution of Anne Colwell, our design manager, to whom we owe our most sincere thanks. Also, our very warm thanks to Meredith Levy for her well-honed editorial skills on Cambridge English Worldwide.

We would also like to thank the Cambridge University Press sales managers and representatives around the world for all their help and support.

Finally, from Andrew, a tribute to Lita, Daniel, Fiona and David for their support and inspiration. From Diana, a big 'thank you' to Tom, Sam and Tara. Thank you for waiting so long.

The authors and publishers would like to thank the following individuals for their vital support throughout the project:

Esteban Cresta, West End School of English, Buenos Aires, Argentina; Silvia Rettaroli and Silvia Luppi, Instituto Superior del Profesorado 'Joaquín V. González' and Minsterio de Cultura y Educación de la Nación, Buenos Aires, Argentina; Beatriz Seveso, María del Carmen Sardi and Ana María Laborde, Supervisión Coordinadora de Idiomas Extranjeros, Secretaría de Educación de la Ciudad de Buenos Aires, Argentina; Nora Carbó, Asociación Rosarina de Cultura Inglesa, Rosario, Argentina; Professor Michael Breen, Edith Cowan University, Perth, Australia; Maria Nina de Andrade Assis, Colégio São Vicente de Paulo, Niterói, Brazil; Thelma Lethier Leite, Instituto Gay-Lussac, Niterói, Brazil; Inés Helena M de Carvalho, Centro Educacional da Lagoa, Rio de Janeiro, Brazil; Maria Claudia F Souza, Colégio da Cidade, Rio de Janeiro, Brazil; Jeff Stranks, Cultura Inglesa, Rio de Janeiro, Brazil; Laura Izarra, OSEC, São Paulo, Brazil; Amine Rassoul, Escola Nova Lourenço Castanho, São Paulo, Brazil; Sergio de Souza Gabriel, Cultura Inglesa, São Paulo, Brazil; Ana Marina Tazoli, Colégio Caminhando, São Paulo, Brazil; Leda Aguiar Vieira, Colégio Bandeirantes, São Paulo, Brazil; Françoise Motard, France; Eleni Miltsakaki, Athens, Greece; Akis Davanellos, The Davanellos School of Languages, Lamia, Greece; Paola Zambonelli, SMS Volta, Bologna, Italy; Cristina Zanoni, SMS Pepoli, Bologna, Italy; Emilia Paloni, SMS Lorenzo Milani, Caivano, Italy; Gisella Langé, Legnano, Italy; Mariella Merli, Milan, Italy; Roberta Fachinetti, SMS Mastri Caravaggini, Caravaggio, Italy; Giovanna Carella, SMS Nazarino Sauro, Novate Milanese, Italy; Dominique Bertrand, SMS Giacomo Leopardi, Rome, Italy; Jan Hague, British Council, Rome, Italy; Val Benson, Suzugamine (Joshi Tandai), Hiroshima, Japan; Małgorzata Szwaj, English Unlimited, Gdańsk, Poland; Alistair MacLean, NKJO, Krosno, Poland; Janina Rybienik, Przemyśl, Poland; Hanna Kijowska, Warsaw, Poland; Ewa Kołodziejska, Warsaw, Poland; Zeynep Çağlar, Beyoğlu Anadolu Lisesi, Istanbul, Turkey; Maureen Günkut, Turkey; Steve Cooke, UK.

The authors and publishers would like to thank the following institutions for their help in testing the material and for the invaluable feedback which they provided:

Colegio Sion, Rio de Janeiro, Brazil; Open English House, Curitiba, Brazil; Ginásio Integrado Madalena Khan, Leblon, Brazil; Steps in English Curso Ltda., Niterói, Brazil; Instituto Educacional Stella Maris, Rio de Janeiro, Brazil; Cultura Inglesa, São Carlos, Brazil; Colegio Bandeirantes, São Paulo, Brazil; Kaumeya Language School, Alexandria, Egypt; Victory College, Victoria, Egypt; Collège Jean Jaures, Aire-sur-la-Lys, France; Collège Louis Le Prince-Ringuet, La Fare-les-Oliviers, France; Collège de Misedon, Port Brillet, France; The Aidonoupolou School, Athens, Greece; the following language school owners in Greece: Petros Dourtourekas, Athens; Eleni Fakalou, Athens; Angeliki & Lance Kinnick, Athens; Mark Palmer, Athens; Georgia Stamatopoulou, Athens; Anna Zerbini-Vasiliadou, Athens; Shirley Papanikolaou, Heraklion; Tony Hatzinikolaou, Kos; Antonis Trechas, Piraeus; SMS Italo Calvino, Milan, Italy; SMS G Rodari, Novate Milanese, Italy; SMS L Fibonacci, Pisa, Italy; Accademia Britannica/International House, Rome, Italy; David English House, Hiroshima, Japan; British Council, Tokyo, Japan; Senri International School, Japan; Szkoła Podstawowa w Bratkówce, Poland; Primary School, Debowiec, Poland; 4th Independent Primary School, Kraków, Poland; Gama Bell School of English, Kraków, Poland; Kosmopolita, Łódź, Poland; Private Language School PRIME, Łódź, Poland; Szkoła Społeczna 2001, Łódź, Poland; Szkoła Podstawowa Nr 11, Nowy Sącz, Poland; Omnibus, Poznań, Poland; Szkoła Języków Obcych J. Rybienik i A. Ochalskiej, Przemyśl, Poland; Szkoła Podstawowa Nr 23, Warsaw, Poland; Szkoła Podstawowa Nr 320, Warsaw, Poland; Liceum Ogólnoksztalcace Wschowa, Poland; Yukselis Koleji I, Ankara, Turkey; Özel Kalamis Lisesi, Istanbul, Turkey; Özel Sener Lisesi, Istanbul, Turkey.

The authors and publishers would like to thank the following for all their help in the production of the finished materials:

Marcus Askwith: freelance design work; Broadway School, Birmingham: help with the *Out and about* photographs. Particular thanks to Martyn Bennett and the children who participated; Peter Ducker: pilot edition design; Gecko Limited, Bicester, Oxon: all stages of design and production. Particular thanks to David Evans, James Arnold, Wendy Homer, Linda Beveridge & Sharon Ryan; Goodfellow & Egan, Cambridge: four-colour scanning and film. Particular thanks to David Ward; Steve Hall of Bell Voice Recordings: recording and production of the songs; Heather Richards: help with selecting artists; Janet and Peter Simmonett: freelance design work; Tim Wharton: writing and performing of songs; Rich Le Page, Diana and Peter Thompson (Studio AVP) and all of the actors who contributed to the recorded material.

The authors and publishers are grateful to the following for permission to record the music and reproduce the words of the following songs:

Wimoweh (The Lion Sleeps Tonight) (words on p. 90): words and music by George David Weiss, Hugo Peretti and Luigi Creatore. Copyright © 1961. Renewed 1989 and assigned to Abilene Music Inc. Administered by The Songwriters Guild of America. Rights for the world, excluding the United States and Canada, controlled by Memory Lane Music Limited, London. All rights reserved – international copyright secured – reprinted by permission.

In My Town, In The Countryside, I Love Chocolate and *Space*: words and music by Tim Wharton. *I'm So Happy* and *Caveman Rock*: words by Andrew Littlejohn & Diana Hicks, music by Tim Wharton.

The authors and publishers are grateful to the following illustrators and photographic sources:

Illustrators: Sophie Allington: pp. 28 t, 29, 30, 40; Felicity Roma Bowers: pp. 31, 35, 84, 85; Maggie Brand: pp. 42 b, 47, 50, 83 t; Robert Calow: pp. 8, 10 t, 15, 16; Richard Deverell: pp. 38, 49, 88; Hilary Evans: handwritten items; Gecko Limited: all DTP illustrations and graphics; Peter Kent: pp. 17, 18 b, 48, 67, 76; Steve Lach: pp. 9, 36, 37, 49, 78; Jan Lewis: all illustrations of recurring exercise markers; Pat Ludlow: pp. 9 t, 12 b, 73, 74, 86; Colin Mier: pp. 41, 60, 63, 82; John Plumb: pp. 20, 53 m, 64 b, 65 b, 68 b, 84 t; Debbie Ryder: pp. 19, 29 b, 44, 66 t, 90, 91, 96 t; Chris Ryley: pp. 64 t, 65 t, 66 b, 68 b, 71, 72, 81, 83 b, 87; John Storey: pp. 8, 10 b, 11, 17, 52, 53 t & b, 54 b, 55, 56, 59; Sam Thompson: p. 42 t; Angela Wood: p. 43; Mel Wright: pp. 14, 18 t, 20 b.

Photographic sources: Aspect Picture Library: p. 52; Aspect Picture Library/ Peter Carmichael: p. 16 mr; Aspect Picture Library/Les Dyson: p. 80 b; Erich Bach/Britstock–IFA: p. 16 t; The J. Allan Cash Photolibrary: pp. 14, 28 bcl, 58, 59 l & r; Bruce Coleman Limited/Bob and Clara Calhoun: p. 34 cr; Bruce Coleman Limited/Rod Williams: p. 34 tr; © 1995 Comstock Inc.: p. 34 cl; Chris Fairclough Colour Library: p. 24 tc; Robert Harding Picture Library: p. 66; Robert Harding Picture Library/Martyn F. Chillmaid: p. 16 ml; Piers Cavendish/Impact Photos: p. 16 mc; NHPA/Stephen Dalton: p. 28 bl; NHPA/Gerard Lacz: p. 30 b; NHPA/Jany Savvanet: p. 34 tl; Pictor International: p. 80 t; Graham Portlock: pp. 16 b, 25, 26, 34 b, 38, 40, 41, 42, 43, 46, 49, 61, 79; Tony Stone Images: pp. 28 tl, tc, tr, bcr & br, 30 t, 70; Zefa Pictures: p. 30 c.

t = top *m* = middle *b* = bottom *r* = right *c* = centre *l* = left

Picture research by Sandie Huskinson-Rolfe of PHOTOSEEKERS.

Cover illustration by Felicity Roma-Bowers.
Cover design by Dunne & Scully.